GOODSON MUMBA

MIND MEETS HEART

The Synergy of Emotional and Intellectual Intelligence

Copyright © 2024 by Goodson Mumba

All rights reserved. No part of this publication may be reproduced, stored or transmitted in any form or by any means, electronic, mechanical, photocopying, recording, scanning, or otherwise without written permission from the publisher. It is illegal to copy this book, post it to a website, or distribute it by any other means without permission.

First edition

ISBN: 9798335328791

This book was professionally typeset on Reedsy. Find out more at reedsy.com

Contents

Preface		iv
Acknowledgement		vii
Dedication		viii
Disclaimer		ix
1	Chapter 1: Introduction to Intelligence	1
2	Chapter 2: Understanding Intellectual Intelligence	21
3	Chapter 3: The Emergence of Emotional Intelligence	38
4	Chapter 4: Comparing IQ and EQ	59
5	Chapter 5: Emotional Intelligence in Leadership	74
6	Chapter 6: Intellectual Intelligence in Problem Solving	92
7	Chapter 7: Emotional Intelligence in Personal Relationships	111
8	Chapter 8: The Workplace: IQ and EQ at Work	131
9	Chapter 9: Education: Teaching for Both IQ and EQ	150
10	Chapter 10: Cultivating Synergy: Practical Applications	171
About the Author		192

Preface

In an age where the pace of change is relentless and the challenges we face are increasingly complex, the need to understand and harness the full spectrum of human intelligence has never been more critical. For too long, our society has placed a disproportionate emphasis on intellectual intelligence—often quantified by IQ scores—while undervaluing the profound impact of emotional intelligence (EQ). This book, *Mind Meets Heart: The Synergy of Emotional and Intellectual Intelligence*, is born out of a deep-seated conviction that true success and fulfillment in life arise from the harmonious integration of these two essential forms of intelligence.

My journey into the exploration of IQ and EQ began with a simple yet powerful question: What does it mean to be truly intelligent? As a lifelong educator, consultant, and advocate for holistic development, I have witnessed firsthand the limitations of an education system that prioritizes cognitive abilities at the expense of emotional and social skills. I have seen brilliant minds struggle with interpersonal relationships, and emotionally astute individuals face challenges in academic settings. This dichotomy, I realized, was not only unnecessary but also detrimental to our collective well-being.

Mind Meets Heart is an invitation to embark on a transformative journey, one that challenges conventional wisdom and opens new avenues for understanding and cultivating intelligence. Through a blend of historical perspectives, scientific research, real-life stories, and practical applications, this book aims to provide a comprehensive framework for integrating IQ and EQ in various spheres of life—from education and leadership to personal relationships and professional development.

In Chapter 1, we lay the foundation by exploring the concept of intelligence from a historical perspective, examining how our understanding has evolved over time. We delve into the traditional view of intellectual intelligence, commonly known as IQ, and why both IQ and EQ matter for a holistic approach to personal and professional success. As we move forward, we will uncover the real-world impacts of IQ and EQ, setting the stage for what to expect throughout the book.

Chapter 2 delves into the depths of intellectual intelligence, tracing its origins, measurement methods, and the intricate interplay between genetics and environment. We will discuss the role of IQ in academic success, address the criticisms of the IQ paradigm, and explore ways to enhance intellectual intelligence.

Chapter 3 shifts our focus to emotional intelligence, drawing upon Daniel Goleman's groundbreaking framework. We will explore the components of EQ, methods for assessing it, and the pivotal role of emotion in decision-making. This chapter will also highlight the importance of EQ in the workplace and offer strategies for improving emotional intelligence.

In Chapter 4, we compare IQ and EQ, highlighting their key differences, strengths, and weaknesses. Through compelling case studies and an exploration of common misconceptions, we will uncover the powerful potential of integrating both forms of intelligence for a balanced and fulfilling life.

Chapters 5 through 8 provide practical insights into the application of IQ and EQ in leadership, problem-solving, personal relationships, and the workplace. We will draw upon real-world examples, case studies, and best practices to illustrate how individuals and organizations can leverage the synergy of IQ and EQ to achieve remarkable outcomes.

Chapter 9 focuses on education, advocating for a paradigm shift that embraces the teaching of both IQ and EQ. We will discuss the importance of integrating EQ into the curriculum, developing intellectual skills in students, and preparing them for a balanced future.

Finally, in Chapter 10, we explore practical strategies for enhancing both IQ and EQ, offering exercises, activities, and real-life success stories. We will provide tools and resources for continued growth, culminating in a vision for the future of intelligence where the synergy of mind and heart is fully realized.

Mind Meets Heart is not just a book; it is a call to action. It is a plea for educators, leaders, parents, and individuals to recognize that intelligence is multifaceted and that true greatness emerges from the harmonious integration of cognitive and emotional capabilities. As you embark on this journey with us, I hope you find inspiration, insight, and practical guidance to enrich your own life and the lives of those around you.

Let us embrace the synergy of emotional and intellectual intelligence and, together, create a brighter, more compassionate, and more intelligent future.

Goodson Mumba

Acknowledgement

I would like to eternally and gratefully acknowledge the Almighty God for the infinite intelligence from His universal mind where we draw from all that we come to know and are yet to know. May I also acknowledge and thank everyone that has played a part in my journey of life in terms of spiritual, moral, emotional and material support.

Dedication

I extend my sincerest gratitude to my beloved wife, Edith Mumba, and our children, Angelina, Lubuto, Letticia, Lulumbi, and Butusho, for their unwavering support and understanding throughout the conception, writing, and eventual publication of this book, despite the sacrifices and challenges they endured.

Disclaimer

This book is a work of fiction. Names, characters, businesses, places, events, and incidents are either the products of the author's imagination or used in a fictitious manner. Any resemblance to actual persons, living or dead, or actual events is purely coincidental.

1

Chapter 1: Introduction to Intelligence

Defining Intelligence: A Historical Perspective

The sun filtered through the tall windows of the lecture hall, casting a warm glow over the room. Dr. Marvis Carter stood at the front, her posture confident yet inviting, as she prepared to address her eager audience of students and professionals alike.

"Intelligence," she began, her voice clear and engaging, "**is a concept that has captivated human thought for centuries. But what exactly is intelligence?**"

She clicked a button on her remote, and an image of ancient philosophers appeared on the screen behind her. "**In the days of Plato and Aristotle,**" she continued, "**intelligence was seen as a divine gift, a spark of the gods that set humans apart from other creatures. It was an abstract, almost mystical quality.**" The audience nodded, some scribbling notes while others sat back, absorbing the information.

Marvis's eyes twinkled as she moved to the next slide, showcasing Renaissance thinkers. **"Fast forward to the Renaissance. Leonardo da Vinci, Galileo – these were not just artists and scientists, but pioneers who believed that intelligence could be cultivated through education and experience. They saw the mind as a muscle, one that could be strengthened through diligent study and exploration."**

She paused, letting the weight of these historical shifts settle in. The room was silent, every eye fixed on her.

"But it was in the 19th century," she said, advancing to a portrait of Francis Galton, **"that the notion of measuring intelligence took root. Galton, often controversial, believed intelligence was hereditary and could be quantified. This led to the birth of the IQ test, a tool that has shaped our understanding of intelligence ever since."**

The students leaned forward, intrigued by the evolution of the concept. **"However,"** Marvis added, **"not everyone agreed with Galton. Alfred Binet, a French psychologist, developed a test not to measure fixed intelligence, but to identify children needing educational assistance. Binet's intention was practical, humanistic – a far cry from Galton's deterministic views."**

She clicked to the next slide, displaying a spectrum of intelligence theories from the 20th century. **"Charles Spearman introduced the idea of 'g' – general intelligence, a single underlying ability. Yet, Howard Gardner challenged this with his theory of multiple intelligences, suggesting that human capability is multi-dimensional, encompassing areas like linguistic, logical-mathematical, spatial, and even musical talents."**

Marvis's voice grew more animated as she reached the

contemporary era. **"And then we have Daniel Goleman's emotional intelligence, or EQ. Goleman argued that self-awareness, empathy, and social skills are just as crucial as cognitive abilities. This marked a paradigm shift, recognizing that intelligence is not solely about what we think, but also about how we feel and interact with others."**

She turned off the projector and faced the audience, her expression thoughtful. **"The history of intelligence,"** she concluded, **"is a tapestry woven with diverse threads of thought and discovery. It teaches us that intelligence is not a static measure, but a dynamic, evolving concept. As we delve deeper into this book, we will explore how the synergy of intellectual and emotional intelligence can unlock our fullest potential."**

The room erupted in applause, the audience electrified by the journey through time and ideas. Dr. Marvis Carter smiled, knowing that this was just the beginning of a profound exploration into the true nature of intelligence.

The Rise of Emotional Intelligence (EQ)

Dr. Marvis Carter stood at the podium, the soft hum of anticipation filling the room. She had just finished discussing the traditional view of intelligence and the importance of intellectual intelligence. Now, she was about to shift the conversation towards a relatively recent yet revolutionary concept—Emotional Intelligence, or EQ.

"We've explored the origins and traditional perspectives on intelligence," Marvis began, her voice carrying a blend of warmth and excitement. **"Now, let's delve into the rise**

of Emotional Intelligence, or EQ, a concept that has transformed our understanding of human potential and performance."

The screen behind her flickered to life, displaying a quote from Daniel Goleman: *"In a very real sense, we have two minds, one that thinks and one that feels."*

"The term 'Emotional Intelligence' was popularized by Daniel Goleman in his groundbreaking book published in 1995," Marvis explained, her eyes scanning the room. "Goleman's work challenged the prevailing notion that IQ alone determines success, introducing the world to the idea that our ability to understand and manage our emotions plays a crucial role in our personal and professional lives."

Marvis then recounted a story, one she had come across during her research. She described a young man named Michael, a brilliant engineer with an IQ that placed him among the top 2% of the population. Despite his intellectual prowess, Michael struggled in his career. His inability to navigate office politics, manage stress, and maintain healthy relationships with colleagues often overshadowed his technical skills.

"Michael's story is not unique," Marvis remarked. "Many individuals with high IQs face similar challenges, highlighting the limitations of relying solely on intellectual intelligence."

The audience nodded in recognition, some exchanging knowing glances.

"This is where Emotional Intelligence comes into play," Marvis continued. "Goleman's framework identified five key components of EQ: self-awareness, self-regulation, motivation, empathy, and social skills. These components enable individuals to navigate the complexities of human interaction, manage their own emotions, and understand the emotions of others."

The screen displayed an infographic of Goleman's five components of EQ, each element illustrated with vibrant colors and icons.

Marvis recounted another story, this time of a woman named Sarah, a school principal who was not only effective in her role but also beloved by students, parents, and staff alike. "**Sarah's success was not just due to her intellectual capabilities but also her exceptional emotional intelligence,**" Marvis explained. "**Her ability to empathize with students, manage conflicts, and inspire her staff made her an exemplary leader.**"

"**The rise of EQ has profound implications for various fields,**" Marvis noted. "**In education, it emphasizes the importance of teaching students emotional and social skills alongside traditional academics. In the workplace, it underscores the need for leaders who can connect with their teams on a deeper level, fostering a positive and productive environment.**"

A hand went up in the back of the room. "Dr. Carter, how can we measure EQ? Is it as straightforward as measuring IQ?"

Marvis smiled, acknowledging the question. "**Measuring EQ is indeed more complex,**" she replied. "**Unlike IQ tests, which provide a numerical score, EQ assessments often involve self-report questionnaires, peer evaluations, and behavioral observations. These tools aim to capture the nuanced and dynamic nature of emotional intelligence.**"

She continued, "**What's important to remember is that while IQ may remain relatively stable throughout life,**

EQ can be developed and enhanced through conscious effort and practice. This is why the rise of EQ is so exciting—it offers us the potential for continuous growth and improvement."

Marvis paused, allowing the weight of her words to settle over the audience. **"As we move forward, we'll explore how the synergy of IQ and EQ can lead to a more holistic and fulfilling approach to success,"** she concluded. **"But first, let's dive deeper into the traditional view of intellectual intelligence, understanding its roots and evolution."**

The room buzzed with a newfound appreciation for Emotional Intelligence, setting the stage for a deeper exploration of how IQ and EQ intersect and complement each other. Dr. Marvis Carter's journey into the realms of human intelligence had only just begun, promising to illuminate paths uncharted and potentials untapped.

The Traditional View: Intellectual Intelligence (IQ)

The applause from Marvis's introductory lecture had barely died down when she moved seamlessly into the next topic. **"Now that we've taken a historical journey, let's focus on the traditional view of intelligence: Intellectual Intelligence, or IQ,"** she announced, her voice resonating with authority.

The slide behind her changed to display a bar graph with the term "IQ" prominently featured. **"Intellectual Intelligence, as many of you know, has long been quantified by the IQ test. But what exactly does IQ measure?"** Marvis asked, her gaze sweeping the room.

A student raised his hand. **"Logical reasoning, mathematical skills, and linguistic ability?"**

"Precisely," Marvis responded, smiling. **"IQ tests assess**

CHAPTER 1: INTRODUCTION TO INTELLIGENCE

a range of cognitive abilities. They aim to measure our capacity to reason, to solve problems, and to understand complex ideas." She pointed to the graph on the screen. "Historically, a high IQ score has been equated with high intelligence. But let's delve deeper."

The slide shifted to an image of Albert Einstein. "**Albert Einstein is often cited as the epitome of high intellectual intelligence. His contributions to physics, particularly the theory of relativity, revolutionized our understanding of the universe. This is a classic example of IQ in action: the ability to think abstractly and solve complex problems.**"

Marvis moved across the stage, the image changing to a bustling classroom. "**But the traditional view doesn't stop there. Educational systems around the world have relied heavily on IQ as a predictor of academic success. Students with high IQs are often placed in advanced classes, given more challenging work, and expected to excel.**" She paused, letting the implications sink in.

A young woman in the front row furrowed her brow. "**Does that mean IQ is the best predictor of success?**" she asked.

Marvis nodded thoughtfully. "**That's a great question. For a long time, many believed so. High IQ was seen as the ticket to academic and professional success. Studies have shown that individuals with higher IQ scores tend to perform better in school and often pursue careers in fields that require strong analytical skills, such as engineering, medicine, and law.**"

She clicked to the next slide, which displayed various IQ test questions. "**These tests typically include tasks like pattern recognition, analogies, and mathematical puzzles. They** are designed to be objective, providing a standardized measure of cognitive ability."

Marvis's expression grew more serious. "**However, this traditional view has its limitations. It tends to overlook other forms of intelligence and skills that are crucial in life but not easily measured by standardized tests. For instance, creativity, practical problem-solving, and interpersonal skills are not adequately captured by IQ tests.**"

The next slide showed a diverse group of people working together in a modern office environment. "**In today's world,**" she continued, "**we need more than just intellectual prowess. The ability to collaborate, communicate effectively, and navigate complex social dynamics is just as important. That's where the concept of Emotional Intelligence comes into play, which we'll explore in greater detail later.**"

Marvis stepped back, her gaze steady and intent. "**The traditional view of intelligence, epitomized by IQ, has given us valuable insights and tools. Yet, it is but one piece of a much larger puzzle. To truly understand and harness our full potential, we must broaden our perspective and consider the myriad ways in which humans can be intelligent.**"

The room was silent, the audience reflecting on the profound complexity of intelligence. Marvis's words had set the stage for a deeper exploration into the balance of intellect and emotion, a journey that would challenge their assumptions and expand their understanding of what it means to be truly intelligent.

CHAPTER 1: INTRODUCTION TO INTELLIGENCE

Why Both Matter: A Holistic Approach

The silence in the lecture hall was palpable as Dr. Marvis Carter paused, allowing her audience a moment to absorb the profound implications of traditional IQ. Then, with a flick of her remote, the screen behind her changed to display two intersecting circles, one labeled "IQ" and the other "EQ."

"We've discussed the traditional view of intellectual intelligence," she began, her voice carrying a note of anticipation. **"Now, let's explore why both IQ and EQ matter and why a holistic approach is essential."**

A buzz of curiosity rippled through the room. Marvis stepped forward, her eyes sweeping the captivated faces. **"Imagine,"** she said, **"a brilliant scientist, someone who excels in logical reasoning and problem-solving. They can decipher the complexities of the universe, but when it comes to collaborating with colleagues or communicating their ideas effectively, they struggle."**

She paused, letting the image settle in the minds of her listeners. **"On the other hand, consider a leader who may not have the highest IQ but possesses a profound ability to understand and manage emotions – their own and those of others. This leader can inspire a team, navigate conflicts, and foster a positive work environment."**

Marvis moved to the side of the stage, revealing a new slide with a quote from Aristotle: **"Educating the mind without educating the heart is no education at all."**

"This quote," she continued, **"captures the essence of why both IQ and EQ are crucial. Intellectual intelligence enables us to understand and manipulate the world around us. It allows us to build, to innovate, to push the** boundaries of what's possible. Emotional intelligence, on the other hand, enables us to connect, to empathize, and to collaborate. It is the glue that binds us together as a society."

The next slide showed a montage of diverse settings: a team of engineers brainstorming, a teacher comforting a student, a doctor reassuring a patient. "**In real-world scenarios,**" Marvis explained, "**we see the need for both types of intelligence. In the workplace, high IQ individuals might develop cutting-edge technologies, but it is those with high EQ who ensure these innovations are implemented effectively, addressing the human aspects of change.**"

A hand shot up in the back row. "**Are there studies that show the impact of combining IQ and EQ?**" a student asked.

"**Absolutely,**" Marvis replied, her face lighting up. "**Research has shown that individuals who score high in both IQ and EQ tend to achieve better outcomes in their personal and professional lives. They are more likely to be successful leaders, effective communicators, and adaptable problem solvers.**"

She clicked to another slide, this one displaying a graph illustrating the correlation between combined high IQ/EQ and job performance. "**In business,**" she said, pointing to the graph, "**leaders who exhibit strong emotional intelligence are more effective in managing teams, driving innovation, and maintaining employee satisfaction. Their intellectual skills provide the foundation for strategic decision-making, while their emotional skills enable them to lead with empathy and vision.**"

Marvis's tone grew more passionate as she moved toward her conclusion. "**A holistic approach to intelligence ac-**

knowledges that our brains and hearts are not isolated entities. They work in concert, each enhancing the other. By cultivating both intellectual and emotional skills, we become more well-rounded, resilient, and capable individuals."

She looked out at her audience, her eyes filled with conviction. "As we progress through this book, we will explore practical ways to develop both types of intelligence. We will learn how to harness the power of our minds and the wisdom of our hearts. Because, ultimately, it is this synergy that allows us to navigate the complexities of life, forge meaningful relationships, and achieve our highest potential."

The room burst into applause, the audience inspired by the vision of a more balanced and integrated approach to intelligence. Dr. Marvis Carter smiled, knowing she had ignited a spark that would guide them through the deeper explorations to come.

Real-World Impacts of IQ and EQ

As the applause subsided, Dr. Marvis Carter clicked the remote again, and the screen transitioned to a bustling cityscape. The vibrant images showed diverse people in various roles: doctors, engineers, artists, teachers, and leaders. Marvis stepped back to the center of the stage, her expression serious yet engaging.

"We've discussed the theoretical importance of both IQ and EQ," she began. "Now, let's examine their real-world impacts. How do these forms of intelligence manifest in our daily lives and careers?"

The first image zoomed in on a high-tech lab. "**Consider**

the field of science and technology," Marvis said. "Here, intellectual intelligence is paramount. **Scientists and engineers with high IQs drive innovation, develop new technologies, and solve complex problems. Their analytical abilities and technical skills push the boundaries of what's possible, leading to breakthroughs that can change the world."**

She clicked to the next slide, which showed a young scientist, Maria, who had recently developed a revolutionary medical device. "**Maria, a brilliant biomedical engineer, exemplifies this impact. Her high IQ allowed her to conceptualize and design a device that can detect diseases at an early stage. Her innovation has the potential to save countless lives.**"

The audience watched intently as Marvis continued. "**However, Maria's journey wasn't without challenges. She faced resistance from investors and skepticism from colleagues. It was her mentor, Dr. Alex Turner, who helped her navigate these hurdles using his high emotional intelligence.**"

The screen shifted to a picture of Alex in a meeting, engaging with colleagues. "**Dr. Turner's EQ enabled him to understand and address the concerns of stakeholders, build strong relationships, and advocate effectively for Maria's project. His empathy and communication skills were crucial in turning Maria's vision into reality.**"

Marvis paused, letting the story resonate. "**This is a perfect example of how IQ and EQ complement each other in the real world. High IQ provided the technical foundation, while high EQ ensured successful implementation and acceptance.**"

CHAPTER 1: INTRODUCTION TO INTELLIGENCE

She moved to another slide, showing a bustling classroom. "In education," she said, "**teachers with high IQ can convey complex information and foster intellectual growth in their students. But it's those with high EQ who truly connect with their students, understand their individual needs, and inspire a love for learning.**"

A video clip played, showing Mrs. Johnson, a beloved high school teacher, engaging with her students. "**Mrs. Johnson combines her deep knowledge of mathematics with her ability to connect emotionally with her students. She recognizes when a student is struggling not just academically, but personally. Her emotional intelligence allows her to provide the support and encouragement her students need to succeed.**"

Marvis smiled at the reactions of her audience, seeing many nodding in agreement. "**In business, the impacts of IQ and EQ are equally significant. CEOs and managers with high IQs drive strategic decisions and innovations. However, those with high EQs excel in leadership, fostering a positive work culture and motivating their teams.**"

She clicked to the next slide, showing a successful business leader, Mark, interacting with his team. "**Mark's company thrived not only because of his sharp business acumen but also because of his ability to understand and manage his team's dynamics. His high EQ helped him to build trust, resolve conflicts, and maintain high morale, which in turn drove productivity and innovation.**"

Marvis took a deep breath, her passion for the subject evident. "**The impacts of IQ and EQ are everywhere, from boardrooms to classrooms, from labs to hospitals. It's the interplay between these two forms of intelligence that** enables individuals and organizations to achieve their full potential."

She concluded with a final image of diverse people coming together, symbolizing unity and collaboration. **"As we move forward, remember that both IQ and EQ are essential. Their real-world impacts show us that true intelligence is not just about being smart or empathetic, but about integrating these qualities to navigate life's complexities and make a meaningful difference."**

The room filled with applause once more, the audience inspired by the tangible examples of how IQ and EQ shape our world. Dr. Marvis Carter smiled, knowing she had conveyed the profound importance of a holistic approach to intelligence, setting the stage for the deeper explorations ahead.

Overview of the Book: What to Expect

As the applause gradually faded, Dr. Marvis Carter walked back to the center of the stage, her demeanor both confident and inviting. She sensed the audience's anticipation, knowing they were eager to understand what the rest of the book had in store for them. She smiled warmly and clicked the remote, revealing a roadmap of the upcoming chapters on the screen.

"Now that we've laid the foundation," Marvis began, **"let's take a moment to look ahead at what this book will cover. Each chapter is designed to deepen our understanding of the synergy between intellectual and emotional intelligence and how it can be harnessed in various aspects of our lives."**

The slide displayed a series of chapter titles, each accompanied by intriguing images. **"In Chapter 2,"** she said, pointing to the first image of a brain and a heart, **"we'll dive into the science behind IQ and EQ. We'll explore the neurological underpinnings of these intelligences and understand how they interact within our brains."**

The next image showed a group of people working together in an office. **"Chapter 3 will take us into the world of education and professional development. We'll examine how combining IQ and EQ can enhance learning experiences and lead to more effective workplace dynamics."**

She continued, her voice rising with enthusiasm. **"In Chapter 4, we'll focus on leadership. We'll hear from successful leaders who've mastered the balance between intellectual and emotional intelligence, and we'll learn practical strategies for leading with both mind and heart."**

The slide transitioned to an image of a serene family scene. **"Chapter 5 will bring us into the realm of personal relationships. We'll discover how IQ and EQ play crucial roles in our interactions with loved ones, friends, and even strangers. We'll discuss communication, empathy, and conflict resolution."**

Marvis glanced at the audience, seeing their rapt attention. **"In Chapter 6, we'll address mental health and well-being. We'll explore how understanding and nurturing both forms of intelligence can lead to a healthier, more balanced life. This chapter will provide tools for managing stress, building resilience, and fostering self-awareness."**

The next image showed a bustling community center. **"Chapter 7 will expand our view to society at large. We'll discuss the broader implications of IQ and EQ in social dynamics, cultural understanding, and global challenges. This chapter will highlight the importance of empathy** and intellectual engagement in creating a more inclusive and compassionate world."

Marvis moved to another slide, which displayed an open book with glowing pages. "**In Chapter 8, we'll look at the future of intelligence. We'll explore emerging trends, technological advancements, and the evolving definitions of intelligence. We'll consider how to prepare ourselves and future generations for a rapidly changing world.**"

The final image showed people of all ages and backgrounds smiling and interacting. "**Finally, in Chapter 9, we'll synthesize everything we've learned. We'll revisit the key insights and offer actionable steps for integrating IQ and EQ into your daily life. This chapter will serve as a practical guide to living a balanced and fulfilling life.**"

Marvis paused, her eyes scanning the room, her voice taking on a tone of encouragement and inspiration. "**This book is not just about understanding intelligence in a theoretical sense. It's about practical application and transformation. My hope is that each chapter will provide you with the knowledge and tools to enhance both your intellectual and emotional capacities.**"

She concluded with a heartfelt statement, her passion palpable. "**By the end of our journey together, I believe you'll see that the synergy of mind and heart is not just a concept, but a powerful approach to navigating life's complexities and achieving true success and fulfillment. Thank you for embarking on this journey with me.**"

The room erupted in applause once more, the audience visibly excited and inspired by the promise of what was to come. Dr. Marvis Carter stepped back, her smile radiant, knowing that she had successfully laid the groundwork for a transformative exploration into the synergy of emotional and intellectual intelligence.

The Origins and Development of IQ

The crisp morning air filled the lecture hall as students settled into their seats, eager for the next chapter of Dr. Marvis Carter's course. The room buzzed with anticipation. Marvis stood at the front, a large chart depicting the evolution of IQ testing displayed behind her.

"**Good morning, everyone,**" Marvis greeted, her voice warm and inviting. "**Today, we embark on a journey through the origins and development of IQ. Let's explore how this concept came to shape our understanding of intellectual intelligence.**"

She clicked a remote, and the screen shifted to an image of a 19th-century classroom. "**Our story begins in the late 1800s with Sir Francis Galton,**" Marvis began. "**Galton was a pioneer in the field of psychometrics. He believed that intelligence was hereditary and could be measured scientifically.**"

The slide transitioned to a portrait of Galton surrounded by statistical charts. "**Galton's work laid the groundwork for the field of intelligence testing. He introduced statistical methods to study human differences and believed that intelligence could be quantified through tests of sensory acuity and reaction times.**"

A student raised his hand. "**So, Galton's focus was more on physical measures of intelligence?**"

"**Exactly,**" Marvis replied. "**But his ideas were revolutionary for their time. He introduced the notion that** intelligence could be measured, which set the stage for future developments."

The screen changed to a bustling Parisian street scene. "**Enter Alfred Binet,**" Marvis continued, her excitement palpable. "**In the early 1900s, the French government commissioned Binet to develop a test that could identify students needing special educational assistance.**"

The slide showed Binet working with children. "**Binet's approach was different. He focused on cognitive abilities rather than sensory measures. His tests assessed memory, attention, and problem-solving skills. Binet believed intelligence was multifaceted and could change with education and experience.**"

Marvis moved across the stage, her movements animated. "**Binet's work culminated in the Binet-Simon scale, the first practical intelligence test. It was designed to identify children who required additional support, not to label them permanently.**"

The next slide displayed the cover of a book: "The Measurement of Intelligence" by Lewis Terman. "**Binet's work caught the attention of American psychologist Lewis Terman, who adapted the Binet-Simon scale for use in the United States. This adaptation became known as the Stanford-Binet Intelligence Test.**"

A video clip played, showing Terman explaining his test to a group of educators. "**Terman believed in the idea of a single, quantifiable intelligence. He introduced the concept of the Intelligence Quotient, or IQ, calculated by dividing a person's mental age by their chronological age and multiplying by 100.**"

The room was silent, the students engrossed in the historical progression. Marvis paused, letting the information sink in before moving on.

"As we moved into the mid-20th century," she continued, "psychologist David Wechsler developed a new intelligence test, the Wechsler Adult Intelligence Scale, or WAIS. Wechsler's test expanded on previous models by including both verbal and performance subtests, providing a more comprehensive view of a person's cognitive abilities."

The slide changed to a diagram of the WAIS components. "Wechsler's contributions highlighted that intelligence was not just a single entity but comprised various skills and abilities. His work emphasized the importance of considering different cognitive domains."

Marvis smiled, sensing the curiosity in the room. "The evolution of IQ testing reflects our growing understanding of human intelligence. From Galton's early experiments to Binet's educational focus, and Terman and Wechsler's comprehensive approaches, each step has contributed to the nuanced view we have today."

A hand went up in the front row. "How do modern IQ tests compare to these early versions?"

Marvis nodded, appreciating the question. "Modern IQ tests, such as the current versions of the Stanford-Binet and the WAIS, build on these foundational ideas but incorporate advancements in psychological research and statistical methods. They are more refined and aim to provide a holistic view of an individual's intellectual capabilities."

She took a deep breath, her tone becoming more reflective. "Understanding the origins and development of IQ helps us appreciate its role and limitations. It's a tool that has evolved over time, shaped by the insights and innovations of many brilliant minds."

Marvis concluded, her voice filled with passion. "As we delve deeper into this book, we will continue to explore how intellectual intelligence intersects with emotional intelligence, and how together, they form a more complete picture of our capabilities."

The room erupted in applause, the students clearly engaged and inspired by the rich history and ongoing evolution of IQ. Dr. Marvis Carter smiled, knowing she had set the stage for a deeper exploration into the complexities of human intelligence.

2

Chapter 2: Understanding Intellectual Intelligence

Measuring Intellectual Intelligence

The excitement from the previous discussion about the origins of IQ still hung in the air as Dr. Marvis Carter prepared to delve into the intricacies of measuring intellectual intelligence. She glanced at the clock, knowing she had to keep the momentum going.

"Now that we've explored the origins and development of IQ," Marvis began, her voice carrying the same enthusiasm, **"let's turn our attention to how intellectual intelligence is measured today. This will help us understand the practical applications and implications of these measurements."**

She clicked the remote, and the screen displayed a series of standardized test booklets and answer sheets. **"Modern IQ tests,"** she continued, **"are sophisticated tools designed to assess a variety of cognitive abilities. The most commonly used tests are the Stanford-Binet Intelligence Scales and** the Wechsler Adult Intelligence Scale, or WAIS."

A student in the back raised her hand. "**What specific skills do these tests measure?**"

Marvis smiled, glad for the question. "**Great question. Let's break it down.**" She clicked to the next slide, which listed several categories.

"**First**," she said, pointing to the list, "**we have verbal comprehension. This includes tasks like vocabulary, similarities, and comprehension questions. These assess how well you understand and use language.**" The screen showed sample questions, such as defining words and explaining similarities between concepts.

The slide shifted to images of puzzles and patterns. "**Next is perceptual reasoning. This measures your ability to solve problems and think abstractly. It includes tasks like block design, matrix reasoning, and visual puzzles. These activities test your non-verbal and spatial reasoning skills.**"

Marvis moved to the next point. "**Working memory is another crucial component. This involves tasks like digit span, where you repeat sequences of numbers, and arithmetic problems that you solve in your head. It measures how well you can hold and manipulate information over short periods.**"

The screen changed again to a stopwatch and rapid-fire questions. "**Then we have processing speed. This assesses how quickly you can process simple or routine information. Tasks like symbol search and coding fall under this category, testing your speed and accuracy.**"

She paused to let the information sink in. "**These categories collectively give us a comprehensive picture of an indi-**

CHAPTER 2: UNDERSTANDING INTELLECTUAL INTELLIGENCE

vidual's intellectual abilities. By combining scores from different areas, we can derive an overall IQ score, which provides a general measure of cognitive function."

A student in the front row, intrigued, asked, "**How reliable and valid are these tests?**"

Marvis nodded, appreciating the depth of the question. "**IQ tests are designed to be both reliable and valid. Reliability means that the test produces consistent results over time. Validity means that the test actually measures what it claims to measure. Extensive research and rigorous statistical methods ensure that these tests meet high standards for both.**"

She clicked to a slide showing a graph of test score distributions. "**The scores are typically distributed in a bell curve, with most people scoring around the average range of 100. Scores between 85 and 115 are considered average. Scores above 130 indicate high intellectual ability, while scores below 70 may suggest challenges that require further support.**"

Marvis's tone grew more reflective as she moved to the next slide, which showed diverse individuals taking tests in various settings. "**It's important to remember that while IQ tests provide valuable insights into cognitive abilities, they are not the sole measure of a person's potential. They capture specific aspects of intelligence but do not encompass the entirety of an individual's capabilities or worth.**"

The screen displayed a quote from Howard Gardner, a prominent psychologist known for his theory of multiple intelligences. "**Gardner's work reminds us that intelligence is multifaceted. IQ tests measure certain cognitive skills, but there are many other forms of intelligence,** such as musical, bodily-kinesthetic, and interpersonal intelligence, that are not captured by traditional IQ tests."

Marvis concluded with a forward-looking statement, her voice filled with optimism. "**As we continue our journey through this book, we will explore how intellectual intelligence interacts with emotional intelligence and other forms of human capability. By understanding and integrating these different aspects, we can develop a more holistic view of intelligence and human potential.**"

The room filled with applause once again, the students clearly engaged and eager to learn more. Dr. Marvis Carter smiled, knowing she had successfully conveyed the complexities and nuances of measuring intellectual intelligence, setting the stage for the next steps in their exploration of the mind and heart.

The Role of Genetics and Environment

The morning sun cast a warm glow through the lecture hall windows as Dr. Marvis Carter stepped back to the podium, the atmosphere charged with anticipation. Her previous discussions had sparked lively debates among the students, and she could sense their eagerness for more.

"**We've delved into the origins and measurement of IQ,**" Marvis began, her voice resonating with enthusiasm. "**Today, we'll explore one of the most fascinating aspects of intellectual intelligence: the interplay between genetics and environment. How much of our intelligence is inherited, and how much is shaped by our surroundings?**"

She clicked the remote, and the screen displayed a family tree, its branches filled with photos of people across generations.

CHAPTER 2: UNDERSTANDING INTELLECTUAL INTELLIGENCE

"Let's start with genetics," she said. "**Research has shown that intelligence has a hereditary component. Studies of twins, especially identical twins, have been crucial in understanding this.**"

A slide popped up showing a pair of identical twins engaged in different activities. "**Identical twins share 100% of their genes. Studies have found that their IQ scores are more similar compared to fraternal twins, who share only 50% of their genes. This suggests a significant genetic influence on intelligence.**"

A student raised his hand. "**But does that mean our IQ is fixed from birth?**"

Marvis shook her head, her expression thoughtful. "**Not at all. While genetics play a role, they are not the sole determinant of intelligence. Environmental factors are equally important. Let's explore this further.**"

The screen transitioned to a bustling classroom scene. "**Education is a critical environmental factor. Access to quality education can significantly impact cognitive development. Children exposed to stimulating environments, with access to books, educational toys, and enriching experiences, tend to develop higher intellectual abilities.**"

Marvis clicked to another slide showing two homes: one filled with books and educational materials, the other sparse and under-resourced. "**Socioeconomic status also plays a crucial role. Children from affluent backgrounds often have more opportunities for intellectual stimulation, while those from impoverished environments may face numerous challenges that hinder their cognitive development.**"

She paused, letting the images sink in. "But it's not just about access to resources. The attitudes and behaviors of caregivers matter too. Supportive and responsive parenting can foster a child's intellectual growth, while neglectful or abusive environments can have detrimental effects."

The next slide showed a brain scan with highlighted areas. "Recent advances in neuroscience have also shed light on the dynamic nature of our brains. Neuroplasticity—the brain's ability to reorganize itself by forming new neural connections—shows that our intellectual abilities can be shaped and reshaped by our experiences throughout life."

A hand went up in the front row. "Can you give an example of how environment and genetics interact?"

Marvis nodded, appreciating the question. "Absolutely. Consider the case of language acquisition. Children are born with the genetic potential for language, but they need an environment rich in linguistic stimuli to develop this ability fully. A child exposed to multiple languages from an early age often becomes proficient in all of them, showcasing how genetic predispositions and environmental factors work together."

She moved to the next slide, which displayed a graph of IQ scores over time. "The Flynn effect is another fascinating example. Over the past century, average IQ scores have been rising globally. This increase is attributed to improvements in education, nutrition, and overall living conditions, underscoring the significant impact of environmental factors."

Marvis's tone grew more passionate as she approached her conclusion. "The interaction between genetics and environment is complex and dynamic. It's not a matter of nature versus nurture but rather how they work together to shape our intellectual abilities. Understanding this interplay can help us create environments that nurture and maximize our potential."

She finished with a final image of diverse people collaborating on a project, symbolizing the combined power of genetic potential and enriching environments. "**As we continue our exploration, we'll see that the synergy between genetics and environment not only affects our intellectual intelligence but also our emotional intelligence and overall well-being. By fostering both, we can achieve a more balanced and fulfilling life.**"

The room erupted in applause, the students clearly inspired and enlightened by the intricate dance between genetics and environment in shaping intelligence. Dr. Marvis Carter smiled, confident that she had deepened their understanding of this critical aspect of human development, paving the way for further discoveries.

IQ and Academic Success

The lecture hall was filled with a sense of eager anticipation as Dr. Marvis Carter prepared to tackle a topic that was especially relevant to her audience of students. She knew that linking IQ to academic success would strike a personal chord, sparking reflections on their own educational journeys.

"**We've examined how genetics and environment shape intellectual intelligence,**" Marvis began, her voice clear and engaging. "**Today, we'll explore the relationship between IQ and academic success. How does IQ influence our** performance in school, and what does it mean for our educational paths?"

She clicked the remote, and the screen displayed an image of a young student taking a standardized test, the familiar Scantron sheet and No. 2 pencil in hand. "**Let's start with the basics,**" she said. "**IQ tests are designed to measure cognitive abilities that are critical for academic achievement: logical reasoning, problem-solving, and understanding complex concepts.**"

The next slide showed a graph correlating IQ scores with academic performance. "**Research consistently shows a positive correlation between IQ and academic success. Students with higher IQ scores tend to perform better on standardized tests, achieve higher grades, and progress more rapidly through school.**"

A student in the middle row raised her hand. "**Does that mean IQ is the best predictor of academic success?**"

Marvis smiled, anticipating the question. "**IQ is a strong predictor, but it's not the only factor. Many other elements contribute to academic success, such as motivation, perseverance, study habits, and emotional support. Let's dive deeper into how IQ interacts with these factors.**"

She clicked to the next slide, which displayed a collage of students engaging in various academic activities: studying in groups, participating in class discussions, and working on projects. "**Students with high IQs often find it easier to grasp new concepts, make connections between ideas, and solve problems efficiently. These abilities can give them an edge in subjects that require critical thinking and analytical skills.**"

The slide changed to show an image of a bustling school

CHAPTER 2: UNDERSTANDING INTELLECTUAL INTELLIGENCE

library. "**However,**" Marvis continued, "**academic success is also about effort and persistence. A student with a high IQ who lacks motivation or doesn't put in the necessary work may not perform as well as a student with a lower IQ who is dedicated and diligent.**"

A video clip played, showing an interview with a high school teacher, Mr. Johnson. "**I've seen students with varying IQ levels excel in my classes,**" Mr. Johnson said. "**The ones who succeed are those who are engaged, curious, and willing to put in the effort. They ask questions, seek help when needed, and are resilient in the face of challenges.**"

Marvis paused the video, letting the teacher's words resonate. "**Mr. Johnson's experience highlights the importance of non-cognitive factors in academic success. Traits like grit, self-discipline, and a growth mindset can significantly impact a student's performance.**"

The screen transitioned to a scene of a student receiving a diploma. "**Moreover,**" Marvis said, "**emotional intelligence plays a crucial role in academic settings. Students who can manage their emotions, build positive relationships, and navigate social complexities are often better equipped to handle the stresses of school life.**"

She moved to a slide showing a diverse group of students celebrating their achievements. "**Supportive relationships with teachers, peers, and family members can enhance a student's academic journey. Emotional support and encouragement can boost a student's confidence and motivation, leading to better academic outcomes.**"

Marvis concluded with a thought-provoking statement, her tone reflective. "**While IQ is an important factor in academic success, it is not the sole determinant. A holistic approach that includes cognitive abilities, emotional intelligence, and personal qualities like perseverance and resilience provides a more comprehensive understanding of what drives academic achievement."

She finished with an image of a bright, open pathway leading to various educational and career opportunities. **"As we continue to explore the synergy between intellectual and emotional intelligence, remember that success is multifaceted. By nurturing both our cognitive and emotional strengths, we can unlock our full potential and achieve our academic and personal goals."**

The room erupted in applause, the students clearly inspired and encouraged by the nuanced understanding of the relationship between IQ and academic success. Dr. Marvis Carter smiled, knowing she had provided them with valuable insights and practical wisdom for their educational journeys.

Criticisms of the IQ Paradigm

The lively discussion from the previous lecture carried over into the next session, filling the room with an undercurrent of excitement. Dr. Marvis Carter stood at the front, ready to address a more contentious aspect of intellectual intelligence: the criticisms of the IQ paradigm. She sensed the curiosity and skepticism in the room, knowing this topic would challenge their perceptions.

"We've covered the strengths and applications of IQ," Marvis began, her tone serious but inviting. **"Today, we'll examine the criticisms of the IQ paradigm. Understanding these criticisms is crucial for a balanced perspective on intelligence."**

CHAPTER 2: UNDERSTANDING INTELLECTUAL INTELLIGENCE

She clicked the remote, and the screen displayed a headline from an old newspaper: "IQ Tests: Controversial Measures of Intelligence." **"IQ testing has been a topic of debate since its inception,"** she continued. **"Let's explore some of the key criticisms that have emerged over the years."**

The first slide showed a diverse group of people taking a standardized test. **"One major criticism is cultural bias,"** Marvis said. **"IQ tests have been accused of favoring certain cultural and socioeconomic groups. Many of the questions reflect the knowledge and experiences of Western, middle-class backgrounds, which can disadvantage those from different cultural or economic environments."**

A student raised his hand. **"Can you give an example of this bias?"**

Marvis nodded, anticipating the question. **"Certainly. Consider a vocabulary question that asks for the definition of a word commonly used in Western literature but not in other cultures. A student unfamiliar with that literature, regardless of their cognitive ability, might struggle with that question."**

The screen transitioned to an image of a crowded, under-resourced classroom. **"Socioeconomic disparities also play a significant role,"** she continued. **"Students from low-income families often have less access to quality education, enrichment activities, and educational materials, which can impact their test performance."**

She clicked to the next slide, which displayed a photo of a frustrated student staring at a complex math problem. **"Another criticism is the narrow focus of IQ tests. They primarily measure analytical and problem-solving skills but often neglect other forms of intelligence, such as** creative, practical, and emotional intelligence."

A short video clip played, showing Dr. Howard Gardner, a renowned psychologist, speaking at a conference. "**In my theory of multiple intelligences,**" Gardner said, "**I argue that we have various kinds of intelligence. Linguistic, logical-mathematical, spatial, musical, bodily-kinesthetic, interpersonal, and intrapersonal intelligences all contribute to our overall capability. IQ tests, however, tend to focus narrowly on just a few of these areas.**"

Marvis paused the video, letting Gardner's words resonate. "**Gardner's theory highlights the limitations of the IQ paradigm in capturing the full spectrum of human intelligence. It reminds us that there's more to intelligence than what traditional tests measure.**"

The next slide showed an old, yellowed IQ test report with the words "Labeled for Life" stamped in red. "**The use of IQ scores to label and categorize individuals is another significant concern,**" Marvis said, her tone somber. "**Labeling someone based on their IQ score can have long-lasting effects on their self-esteem and opportunities. It can lead to a fixed mindset, where individuals believe their abilities are static and unchangeable.**"

A student in the front row asked, "**What about the role of effort and growth mindset in intelligence?**"

Marvis's eyes brightened. "**Great point. Research by psychologist Carol Dweck has shown that a growth mindset—believing that abilities can be developed through hard work and perseverance—can lead to greater achievement and resilience. Overemphasizing IQ scores can undermine this mindset, making people feel limited by their initial assessments.**"

CHAPTER 2: UNDERSTANDING INTELLECTUAL INTELLIGENCE

The slide changed to a graph showing the distribution of IQ scores and the Flynn effect. **"Finally, we must consider the Flynn effect, which we discussed earlier. The consistent rise in average IQ scores over the past century suggests that IQ is not a fixed trait but can be influenced by environmental factors such as education, nutrition, and social changes."**

Marvis concluded with a thought-provoking statement, her tone reflective and inclusive. **"Criticisms of the IQ paradigm remind us that intelligence is a complex, multifaceted phenomenon. While IQ tests provide valuable insights, they are not the definitive measure of a person's intellectual capabilities. We must consider the broader context, including cultural, environmental, and personal factors, to understand and nurture the full potential of every individual."**

She finished with an image of a diverse group of people engaging in various activities—learning, creating, collaborating—symbolizing the richness and diversity of human intelligence. **"As we move forward, we'll continue to explore how integrating different forms of intelligence, both intellectual and emotional, can lead to a more comprehensive and fulfilling understanding of our potential."**

The room erupted in applause, the students clearly moved and inspired by the critical examination of the IQ paradigm. Dr. Marvis Carter smiled, knowing she had deepened their understanding and encouraged them to think more broadly about intelligence and human capability.

Enhancing Intellectual Intelligence

The room buzzed with anticipation as Dr. Marvis Carter returned to the podium. After exploring the complexities and criticisms of IQ, the students were eager to learn about ways to enhance their own intellectual intelligence. Marvis sensed their excitement and prepared to share practical strategies and inspiring stories.

"**Good afternoon, everyone,**" Marvis began, her voice warm and engaging. "**Today, we'll focus on enhancing intellectual intelligence. While IQ is often seen as a fixed trait, there are numerous ways to boost our cognitive abilities and unlock greater potential.**"

She clicked the remote, and the screen displayed an image of a young woman reading a book under a tree. "**Let's start with lifelong learning,**" Marvis said. "**Engaging in continuous education, whether formal or informal, stimulates the brain and fosters intellectual growth. Reading widely, taking up new hobbies, and enrolling in courses can all contribute to cognitive development.**"

A student raised his hand. "**Can you give an example of how a new hobby can enhance intelligence?**"

Marvis nodded, appreciating the question. "**Absolutely. Consider learning a musical instrument. It involves reading music, coordinating movements, and understanding rhythm and pitch. This not only enhances auditory and motor skills but also improves memory and problem-solving abilities.**"

The next slide showed a group of students working on a complex project. "**Collaboration and social interaction are also key,**" she continued. "**Engaging in discussions, working in

CHAPTER 2: UNDERSTANDING INTELLECTUAL INTELLIGENCE

teams, and participating in intellectual debates challenge our thinking and expose us to diverse perspectives. This can deepen our understanding and spark new ideas."

A short video clip played, showing students at a debate competition. One of the participants, Sarah, shared her experience. "Debating has taught me to think critically and articulate my thoughts clearly. It's not just about winning arguments but about understanding different viewpoints and refining my own beliefs."

Marvis paused the video, letting Sarah's words resonate. "Sarah's experience highlights the value of intellectual engagement with others. It sharpens our thinking and helps us learn from each other."

The screen transitioned to a serene scene of a person meditating. "Mental and physical health also play crucial roles," Marvis said. "Practices like mindfulness and meditation can improve focus, reduce stress, and enhance cognitive function. Regular physical exercise boosts blood flow to the brain, promoting neural health and improving memory and learning."

A hand went up in the back row. "How can mindfulness improve cognitive abilities?"

Marvis smiled. "Mindfulness trains the brain to focus and stay present. Studies have shown that regular mindfulness practice can increase gray matter density in areas of the brain associated with learning, memory, and emotional regulation. It helps us become more aware of our thoughts and more effective in managing them."

The next slide displayed a balanced plate of nutritious food. "Nutrition is another important factor," she continued. "A diet rich in fruits, vegetables, whole grains, and lean proteins provides the essential nutrients that support brain function. Omega-3 fatty acids, found in fish and flaxseeds, are particularly beneficial for cognitive health."

Marvis's tone grew more reflective as she approached her conclusion. "**It's also essential to challenge ourselves intellectually. Engaging in activities that push our cognitive limits, such as learning a new language, solving puzzles, or mastering a new skill, keeps our brains active and adaptable.**"

The screen showed an image of a person writing in a journal. "**Finally, setting goals and reflecting on our progress can help us stay motivated and focused. Keeping a journal of our learning experiences, challenges, and achievements can provide valuable insights and a sense of accomplishment.**"

Marvis concluded with a thought-provoking statement, her voice filled with encouragement. "**Enhancing intellectual intelligence is an ongoing journey. By embracing lifelong learning, engaging with others, maintaining our mental and physical health, and continually challenging ourselves, we can unlock our full cognitive potential and achieve greater success in all areas of life.**"

She finished with an image of a bright, open pathway leading to various educational and personal growth opportunities. "**As we continue to explore the synergy between intellectual and emotional intelligence, remember that both can be nurtured and developed. By fostering these aspects of ourselves, we can lead richer, more fulfilling lives.**"

The room filled with applause, the students clearly inspired by the practical strategies for enhancing their intellectual intelligence. Dr. Marvis Carter smiled, knowing she had provided them with valuable tools and motivation for their journey of lifelong learning and personal growth.

3

Chapter 3: The Emergence of Emotional Intelligence

The Concept of EQ: Goleman's Framework

The atmosphere in the lecture hall was one of curiosity and anticipation. Dr. Marvis Carter stood at the front, ready to introduce a topic that had revolutionized the understanding of human intelligence: Emotional Intelligence, or EQ. She knew this would be a pivotal moment in their journey.

"**Good morning, everyone,**" Marvis began, her voice full of enthusiasm. "**Today, we're diving into Emotional Intelligence, often referred to as EQ. This concept, popularized by psychologist Daniel Goleman, has transformed how we think about intelligence and its role in our lives.**"

She clicked the remote, and the screen displayed a photograph of Daniel Goleman, smiling warmly. "**Goleman's work on Emotional Intelligence,**" Marvis continued, "**has shown us that being smart isn't just about having a high IQ. It's**

CHAPTER 3: THE EMERGENCE OF EMOTIONAL INTELLIGENCE

also about understanding and managing our emotions and those of others."

The next slide featured the cover of Goleman's seminal book, *Emotional Intelligence*, with the subtitle: "Why It Can Matter More Than IQ." "**In 1995, Goleman's book brought the concept of EQ to the mainstream,**" Marvis said. "**He argued that emotional intelligence is a critical factor in personal and professional success, often outweighing traditional cognitive intelligence.**"

A student in the front row raised her hand. "**What exactly is emotional intelligence?**"

Marvis nodded, glad for the opportunity to elaborate. "**Great question. Goleman defines EQ as the ability to recognize, understand, and manage our own emotions, as well as the ability to recognize, understand, and influence the emotions of others. He breaks it down into five key components.**"

The screen transitioned to a diagram illustrating Goleman's five components of EQ. "**Let's go through each of these components,**" Marvis said, pointing to the first section of the diagram.

"**Self-awareness is the first component,**" she explained. "**It's about being aware of our own emotions, recognizing how they affect our thoughts and behavior, and understanding our strengths and weaknesses. This awareness helps us navigate our emotional landscape with greater clarity.**"

A short video clip played, showing an interview with a business leader, Jessica, who shared her experience. "**Self-awareness has been crucial in my career,**" Jessica said. "**By understanding my emotional triggers, I can manage stress** better and make more thoughtful decisions."

Marvis paused the video, letting Jessica's words resonate. "**Jessica's story highlights the importance of self-awareness in achieving emotional balance and professional success,**" she said.

She clicked to the next component: self-regulation. "**Self-regulation is about managing our emotions effectively,**" Marvis continued. "**It involves controlling impulsive behaviors, thinking before acting, and staying calm under pressure. This helps us maintain composure and adapt to changing circumstances.**"

The next slide showed a serene image of a person practicing mindfulness. "**Mindfulness and emotional regulation go hand in hand,**" Marvis noted. "**Techniques like deep breathing and meditation can help us stay grounded and manage our emotional responses more effectively.**"

A student in the middle row asked, "**How does self-regulation impact our interactions with others?**"

Marvis smiled. "**Excellent question. Self-regulation not only helps us manage our own emotions but also influences how we respond to others. It fosters patience, empathy, and thoughtful communication, which are essential for building strong relationships.**"

The screen then displayed a group of people engaged in a lively discussion. "**Next, we have motivation,**" Marvis said. "**This is the drive to achieve our goals, even in the face of setbacks. It's about having a passion for what we do and staying committed to our objectives. Intrinsic motivation, driven by internal rewards, often leads to greater satisfaction and success.**"

A hand went up in the back row. "**Can you give an example

CHAPTER 3: THE EMERGENCE OF EMOTIONAL INTELLIGENCE

of intrinsic motivation?"

Marvis nodded. "Certainly. **Imagine a teacher who loves educating and inspiring students. Their motivation comes from the joy of teaching and seeing their students succeed, rather than external rewards like salary or recognition. This intrinsic motivation fuels their passion and effectiveness.**"

The next slide focused on empathy. "**Empathy is the ability to understand and share the feelings of others,**" Marvis explained. "**It's about seeing things from another person's perspective and responding with compassion. Empathy strengthens our connections with others and enhances our ability to collaborate and support each other.**"

A short clip played, showing a nurse, Maria, talking about her experience. "**Empathy is at the heart of my work,**" Maria said. "**By truly understanding my patients' emotions, I can provide better care and comfort.**"

Marvis paused the video, her tone thoughtful. "**Maria's experience underscores the vital role of empathy in building trust and fostering positive relationships.**"

Finally, the screen displayed a team celebrating a successful project. "**The last component is social skills,**" Marvis said. "**These are the skills we use to interact and communicate with others effectively. Good social skills help us build networks, resolve conflicts, and work collaboratively. They are essential for leadership and teamwork.**"

Marvis concluded with a reflective statement, her voice filled with optimism. "**Goleman's framework of Emotional Intelligence shows us that managing our emotions and understanding those of others are crucial for personal and professional success. As we continue our journey,** we'll explore how EQ complements IQ, creating a powerful synergy that enhances every aspect of our lives."

The room filled with applause, the students clearly inspired and eager to learn more about the transformative power of Emotional Intelligence. Dr. Marvis Carter smiled, knowing she had sparked a new level of curiosity and understanding in their exploration of the mind and heart.

Components of Emotional Intelligence

The air was thick with anticipation as the students settled back into their seats. Dr. Marvis Carter could feel the energy in the room. Today, she would delve deeper into the specific components of Emotional Intelligence (EQ) that Daniel Goleman had outlined. This session would provide them with a comprehensive understanding of how each component contributes to overall emotional intelligence.

"**Welcome back, everyone,**" Marvis began, her tone both warm and invigorating. "**In our last session, we introduced the concept of Emotional Intelligence and Goleman's framework. Today, we'll break down the five components of EQ in detail: self-awareness, self-regulation, motivation, empathy, and social skills.**"

She clicked the remote, and the screen displayed a mind map with five branches, each labeled with one of the EQ components. "**Let's start with self-awareness,**" Marvis said. "**This is the foundation of emotional intelligence. Self-awareness involves recognizing and understanding our own emotions, as well as how they affect our thoughts and behavior.**"

A short video clip played, showing a young woman, Rachel,

CHAPTER 3: THE EMERGENCE OF EMOTIONAL INTELLIGENCE

reflecting on her emotions in a journal. **"Writing in my journal helps me understand my feelings better,"** Rachel said. **"It's like having a conversation with myself, where I can explore my emotions and reactions."**

Marvis paused the video, allowing Rachel's words to sink in. **"Rachel's practice of journaling is a powerful tool for enhancing self-awareness,"** she noted. **"By regularly reflecting on our emotions, we can gain insights into our triggers and patterns, helping us navigate our emotional landscape more effectively."**

The next slide displayed an image of a calm person taking deep breaths. **"Self-regulation is the next component,"** Marvis continued. **"It's about managing our emotions and impulses in healthy ways. This includes controlling our reactions, staying composed under pressure, and maintaining a positive outlook."**

A student raised his hand. **"How can we improve self-regulation in our daily lives?"**

Marvis smiled, pleased with the engagement. **"Great question. Techniques such as mindfulness meditation, deep breathing exercises, and cognitive reframing can help. For example, when we encounter a stressful situation, taking a few deep breaths can help us regain control and respond more calmly."**

The screen transitioned to a scene of a runner crossing the finish line, sweat and determination etched on their face. **"Motivation is the third component,"** Marvis said. **"It's the drive to achieve our goals for reasons beyond external rewards. Intrinsic motivation, fueled by personal passion and commitment, is particularly powerful."**

A clip played of an entrepreneur, Alex, sharing his story.

"Starting my own business was challenging," Alex said. "But my passion for creating innovative products kept me going, even when things got tough. That internal drive made all the difference."

Marvis paused the video. "**Alex's experience illustrates the importance of motivation in achieving long-term goals. When we're driven by our own passions and values, we're more resilient and persistent.**"

The next slide featured a compassionate nurse comforting a patient. "**Empathy is the fourth component,**" Marvis continued. "**It's the ability to understand and share the feelings of others. Empathy allows us to connect with people on a deeper level, fostering trust and collaboration.**"

A hand went up in the back row. "**Can you give an example of empathy in action?**"

Marvis nodded. "**Certainly. Imagine a manager who notices an employee is struggling. Instead of criticizing their performance, the manager takes the time to listen and understand what's going on. By showing empathy, the manager can offer support and help the employee find solutions, strengthening their relationship and improving workplace morale.**"

The final slide displayed a group of people working together harmoniously. "**Lastly, we have social skills,**" Marvis said. "**These are the skills we use to interact with others effectively. Good social skills help us communicate clearly, resolve conflicts, and build strong relationships.**"

A video clip showed a team leader, Mark, facilitating a meeting. "**Effective communication and active listening are key,**" Mark explained. "**By ensuring everyone feels heard and valued, we can work together more effectively** and achieve our goals."

Marvis concluded with a reflective statement, her voice filled with encouragement. **"Goleman's components of Emotional Intelligence provide us with a comprehensive framework for understanding and enhancing our emotional capabilities. By developing self-awareness, self-regulation, motivation, empathy, and social skills, we can improve our personal and professional lives, creating a more fulfilling and harmonious existence."**

She finished with an image of a tree with roots and branches labeled with the EQ components, symbolizing growth and interconnectedness. **"As we continue to explore Emotional Intelligence, remember that each component is vital to our overall well-being. By nurturing these aspects of ourselves, we can achieve greater emotional balance and success."**

The room filled with applause, the students clearly inspired and eager to apply the principles of Emotional Intelligence in their own lives. Dr. Marvis Carter smiled, knowing she had provided them with valuable insights and practical tools for their journey toward emotional and intellectual synergy.

Assessing Emotional Intelligence

The class buzzed with an undercurrent of curiosity as Dr. Marvis Carter returned to the podium. The students were eager to learn how to measure the abstract and often elusive concept of Emotional Intelligence. Dr. Carter knew this session would equip them with practical tools to understand their own and others' emotional capabilities.

"Welcome back, everyone," Marvis began, her voice infused with enthusiasm. "Today, we'll delve into assessing Emotional Intelligence. Just as we have tools to measure IQ, there are ways to evaluate EQ, providing valuable insights into our emotional skills and areas for growth."

She clicked the remote, and the screen displayed a colorful chart with various assessment methods. "There are several ways to assess Emotional Intelligence," she continued. "These include self-report questionnaires, performance-based tests, and 360-degree feedback. Each method has its own strengths and can offer different perspectives on our emotional capabilities."

The first slide showed an image of a person filling out a survey. "Self-report questionnaires are one of the most common methods," Marvis explained. "These surveys ask individuals to rate themselves on various aspects of emotional intelligence. While they provide useful self-reflection, they can be influenced by personal biases."

A student in the front row raised her hand. "Can you give an example of a self-report questionnaire?"

Marvis nodded, anticipating the question. "Sure. One well-known example is the Emotional Quotient Inventory (EQ-i), developed by psychologist Reuven Bar-On. It assesses various components of EQ, such as self-awareness, stress management, and interpersonal skills, through a series of statements that individuals rate based on their agreement."

The screen transitioned to a graphic of a person performing a task on a computer. "Performance-based tests offer a more objective measure," Marvis said. "These tests assess emotional intelligence through specific tasks that evaluate emotional understanding and management. One such

tool is the Mayer-Salovey-Caruso Emotional Intelligence Test (MSCEIT)."

A short video clip played, showing Dr. John Mayer discussing the MSCEIT. **"The MSCEIT measures how well people can perceive, use, understand, and manage emotions,"** Mayer explained. **"Participants are given scenarios and asked to identify emotions, reason with emotions, and solve emotion-related problems."**

Marvis paused the video, letting Mayer's words resonate. **"Performance-based tests like the MSCEIT provide valuable insights into how we apply emotional intelligence in real-life situations,"** she noted.

The next slide displayed a team in a collaborative meeting. **"360-degree feedback is another powerful method,"** Marvis continued. **"This involves gathering feedback from peers, subordinates, and supervisors to get a well-rounded view of an individual's emotional intelligence. It highlights how others perceive our emotional skills and can identify areas for improvement that we might not see ourselves."**

A hand went up in the middle row. **"How does 360-degree feedback work in practice?"**

Marvis smiled, appreciating the engagement. **"Great question. In practice, participants receive feedback from multiple sources using structured questionnaires. This feedback is then compiled into a comprehensive report, highlighting strengths and areas for growth. It's often used in leadership development to enhance emotional and social competencies."**

The screen then showed a chart with various EQ scores and their implications. **"Interpreting these assessments requires understanding what the scores mean,"** Marvis said.

"**High scores in self-awareness might indicate a strong ability to recognize and understand one's emotions, while lower scores in self-regulation might suggest challenges in managing emotional responses.**"

A clip played of a human resources manager, Lisa, explaining how her organization uses EQ assessments. "**We use EQ assessments as part of our professional development programs,**" Lisa said. "**They help employees understand their emotional strengths and areas for improvement, leading to more effective communication and teamwork.**"

Marvis paused the video, her tone reflective. "**Lisa's experience illustrates how EQ assessments can be used to foster personal and professional growth. By understanding our emotional intelligence, we can develop strategies to enhance our skills and improve our interactions with others.**"

The final slide displayed an image of a person standing in front of a mirror, symbolizing self-reflection. "**Ultimately, assessing Emotional Intelligence is about gaining insights and taking action,**" Marvis concluded. "**Whether through self-report questionnaires, performance-based tests, or 360-degree feedback, these assessments provide valuable information to help us grow and improve.**"

She finished with a thought-provoking statement, her voice filled with encouragement. "**As we continue to explore Emotional Intelligence, remember that assessment is just the beginning. The true value lies in using these insights to enhance our emotional skills, leading to more fulfilling relationships and successful endeavors.**"

The room filled with applause, the students clearly inspired and eager to apply what they had learned about assessing their emotional intelligence. Dr. Marvis Carter smiled, knowing she had provided them with essential tools for their journey of emotional and intellectual growth.

The Role of Emotion in Decision Making

The students settled back into their seats, the hum of conversation dying down as Dr. Marvis Carter prepared to delve into the next intriguing aspect of Emotional Intelligence: the role of emotion in decision making. Marvis knew that this topic would challenge their understanding of how decisions are made and highlight the profound impact of emotions on their choices.

"**Welcome back,**" Marvis began, her voice lively and engaging. "**Today, we'll explore how emotions influence our decision-making processes. While we often think of decisions as purely rational, emotions play a crucial role, guiding and shaping our choices in ways we might not always realize.**"

She clicked the remote, and the screen displayed a picture of a brain divided into emotional and rational sections. "**Neuroscience has shown that our brains are wired to integrate emotional and rational inputs when making decisions,**" Marvis explained. "**The limbic system, which processes emotions, and the prefrontal cortex, responsible for rational thinking, work together to help us navigate complex choices.**"

A student in the front row raised his hand. "**Can you give an example of how emotions influence a decision?**"

Marvis nodded, anticipating the question. "**Absolutely. Consider a job offer. The rational part of your brain evalu-**

ates the salary, benefits, and career prospects. Meanwhile, your emotions might weigh the company culture, your excitement about the role, or anxiety about relocation. Both rational analysis and emotional response shape your final decision."

The next slide showed a decision-making flowchart with emotions intertwined at each step. "**Emotions provide valuable information that can enhance our decision-making,**" Marvis continued. "**They signal what matters to us, highlight potential risks, and drive our motivations. For instance, a gut feeling might alert us to something we haven't consciously noticed.**"

A short video clip played, featuring Dr. Antonio Damasio, a prominent neuroscientist, discussing his research. "**Our emotions are integral to decision-making,**" Damasio explained. "**Without them, we would struggle to make choices, even in simple situations. Emotions guide our reasoning and help us prioritize.**"

Marvis paused the video, letting Damasio's words sink in. "**Dr. Damasio's research illustrates the necessity of emotions in making effective decisions,**" she said. "**Far from being a hindrance, emotions enrich our decision-making processes, adding depth and insight.**"

The next slide displayed an image of a person faced with two diverging paths. "**Emotional intelligence helps us harness the power of our emotions in decision-making,**" Marvis noted. "**By recognizing and understanding our emotions, we can use them constructively rather than letting them overwhelm us or lead us astray.**"

A hand went up in the middle row. "**How can we improve our emotional intelligence to make better decisions?**"

CHAPTER 3: THE EMERGENCE OF EMOTIONAL INTELLIGENCE

Marvis smiled, appreciating the engagement. "**Great question. Enhancing emotional intelligence involves developing self-awareness, self-regulation, and empathy. By being aware of our emotions, we can pause and reflect before making decisions. Techniques such as mindfulness and emotional journaling can help us understand our emotional responses and use them wisely.**"

The screen transitioned to a scenario of a team making a strategic business decision. "**In professional settings, leaders with high emotional intelligence can make more balanced decisions by considering both data and the emotional climate of their team,**" Marvis said. "**They are better equipped to handle stress, manage conflicts, and inspire their teams.**"

A clip played of a CEO, David, discussing his approach to decision-making. "**Understanding my team's emotions and motivations has been crucial,**" David said. "**It helps me make decisions that are not only strategically sound but also resonate with my team, fostering a positive and productive work environment.**"

Marvis paused the video, her tone reflective. "**David's experience highlights the impact of emotional intelligence on leadership and organizational success. By integrating emotional insights with rational analysis, leaders can create more effective and harmonious workplaces.**"

The final slide displayed an image of a balanced scale, symbolizing the integration of emotion and reason. "**Ultimately, the role of emotion in decision-making is about finding balance,**" Marvis concluded. "**By acknowledging and understanding our emotions, we can use them to inform and enhance our rational decisions. This holistic** approach leads to more thoughtful, well-rounded choices in both our personal and professional lives."

She finished with a thought-provoking statement, her voice filled with encouragement. "**As we continue to explore Emotional Intelligence, remember that emotions are not obstacles but allies in our decision-making journey. By embracing our emotional insights, we can make decisions that are not only smart but also deeply aligned with our values and aspirations.**"

The room filled with applause, the students clearly inspired and eager to apply what they had learned about the role of emotion in decision-making. Dr. Marvis Carter smiled, knowing she had provided them with essential tools for their journey toward emotional and intellectual synergy.

EQ in the Workplace

As the class settled in, Dr. Marvis Carter stood at the front, ready to explore the transformative power of Emotional Intelligence (EQ) in the workplace. She knew that understanding how EQ influences professional interactions would be crucial for her students' future success.

"**Good afternoon, everyone,**" Marvis greeted, her voice projecting warmth and enthusiasm. "**Today, we'll dive into how Emotional Intelligence shapes the dynamics of the workplace. From leadership to team collaboration, EQ plays a pivotal role in fostering a positive and productive work environment.**"

She clicked the remote, and the screen displayed a bustling office scene with employees engaged in various tasks. "**Emotional Intelligence is increasingly recognized as a critical** skill in the workplace," Marvis explained. "**It influences how we communicate, collaborate, and lead others, ultimately impacting organizational culture and success.**"

The next slide showcased a diagram depicting the components of EQ intertwined with professional scenarios. "**Let's explore how each component of Emotional Intelligence manifests in the workplace,**" Marvis continued. "**From self-awareness to social skills, these competencies are essential for navigating the complexities of professional relationships.**"

The first scenario displayed an employee receiving constructive feedback from their manager. "**Self-awareness is the foundation of effective leadership,**" Marvis noted. "**Leaders who are self-aware understand their strengths, weaknesses, and how their actions impact others. This awareness allows them to adapt their leadership style and foster a culture of growth and development.**"

A hand went up in the front row. "**How can leaders enhance their self-awareness?**"

Marvis nodded, appreciating the question. "**Leaders can cultivate self-awareness through practices such as reflective journaling, seeking feedback from others, and engaging in mindfulness exercises. By regularly reflecting on their thoughts and behaviors, leaders can gain insights into their leadership approach and its impact on their team.**"

The next slide featured a team collaborating on a project, showcasing effective communication and cooperation. "**Social skills are another key component of Emotional Intelligence in the workplace,**" Marvis explained. "**Employees with strong social skills excel in building relationships,** resolving conflicts, and fostering teamwork. They create a supportive and inclusive work environment where everyone feels valued and heard."

A short video clip played, featuring a team leader facilitating a brainstorming session. "**Clear communication and active listening are essential for effective collaboration,**" the team leader emphasized. "**By creating an open and respectful environment, we encourage diverse perspectives and innovative solutions.**"

Marvis paused the video, her tone reflective. "**The team leader's approach highlights the importance of social skills in driving team performance and achieving collective goals,**" she noted.

The next slide displayed a manager providing support to an employee during a challenging project. "**Empathy is a cornerstone of effective leadership and employee engagement,**" Marvis continued. "**Managers who demonstrate empathy understand their employees' perspectives, emotions, and needs. They provide support, encouragement, and constructive feedback, fostering a culture of trust and psychological safety.**"

A hand went up in the middle row. "**How can managers cultivate empathy in the workplace?**"

Marvis smiled, pleased with the engagement. "**Managers can cultivate empathy by actively listening to their employees, practicing perspective-taking, and demonstrating empathy in their interactions. By showing genuine care and understanding, managers can build stronger relationships with their team members and create a supportive work environment.**"

The final slide showcased a diverse team celebrating a

successful project completion. **"Ultimately, Emotional Intelligence is a catalyst for organizational success,"** Marvis concluded. **"By cultivating self-awareness, social skills, and empathy, leaders and employees can create a workplace culture that fosters collaboration, innovation, and employee well-being. This not only enhances productivity but also contributes to long-term growth and success."**

She finished with a thought-provoking statement, her voice filled with encouragement. **"As we continue to explore Emotional Intelligence in the workplace, remember that each interaction presents an opportunity to practice and develop these essential skills. By prioritizing EQ, we can create workplaces where everyone can thrive and contribute their best."**

The room filled with applause, the students clearly inspired and eager to apply what they had learned about EQ in the workplace. Dr. Marvis Carter smiled, knowing she had provided them with valuable insights for their future careers.

Strategies to Improve Emotional Intelligence

As the class settled in, Dr. Marvis Carter stood at the front, ready to equip her students with practical strategies to enhance their Emotional Intelligence (EQ). She knew that fostering the development of EQ would empower them to navigate the complexities of emotions both in their personal and professional lives.

"Good afternoon, everyone," Marvis greeted, her voice brimming with enthusiasm. **"Today, we'll explore actionable strategies to improve our Emotional Intelligence. By implementing these techniques, we can cultivate greater**

self-awareness, enhance our relationships, and achieve success in various aspects of life."

She clicked the remote, and the screen displayed a roadmap with steps to enhance EQ. **"Improving Emotional Intelligence requires intentional effort and practice,"** Marvis explained. **"These strategies focus on developing key EQ competencies such as self-awareness, self-regulation, empathy, and social skills."**

The first strategy highlighted the importance of self-reflection and introspection. **"Self-awareness begins with introspection,"** Marvis noted. **"Taking time for self-reflection allows us to explore our thoughts, emotions, and behaviors. Journaling, meditation, and mindfulness exercises are effective tools for enhancing self-awareness and gaining insights into our inner world."**

A hand went up in the front row. **"How can we incorporate self-reflection into our daily routines?"**

Marvis nodded, appreciating the question. **"Great question. You can start by setting aside a few minutes each day for quiet reflection. Find a peaceful environment where you can be alone with your thoughts. You may also find it helpful to jot down your reflections in a journal or use guided meditation apps to facilitate the process."**

The next slide showcased strategies for self-regulation and managing emotions effectively. **"Self-regulation involves recognizing and controlling our emotional responses,"** Marvis explained. **"Techniques such as deep breathing, progressive muscle relaxation, and cognitive reframing can help us manage stress, reduce anxiety, and maintain emotional balance in challenging situations."**

A short video clip played, featuring a psychologist demonstrating deep breathing exercises. "**Deep breathing is a simple yet powerful technique for calming the mind and body,**" the psychologist explained. "**By focusing on your breath, you can reduce physiological arousal and regain control over your emotions.**"

Marvis paused the video, her tone reflective. "**Deep breathing is just one example of a self-regulation technique,**" she noted. "**Experiment with different strategies to find what works best for you.**"

The next slide displayed strategies for cultivating empathy and building stronger relationships. "**Empathy is the ability to understand and share the feelings of others,**" Marvis continued. "**To enhance empathy, practice active listening, perspective-taking, and nonverbal communication. Show genuine interest in others' experiences and emotions, and seek to understand their perspectives without judgment.**"

A hand went up in the middle row. "**How can we improve our nonverbal communication skills?**"

Marvis smiled, pleased with the engagement. "**Nonverbal communication plays a significant role in conveying empathy and building rapport,**" she explained. "**Practice maintaining eye contact, using open body language, and mirroring the emotions of others. Pay attention to subtle cues such as facial expressions and gestures, as they can provide valuable insights into someone's emotional state.**"

The final slide showcased strategies for developing strong social skills and fostering meaningful connections. "**Social skills are essential for building and maintaining relationships,**" Marvis concluded. "**To enhance social skills, practice effective communication, conflict resolution,** and teamwork. **Seek opportunities to collaborate with others, volunteer in group settings, and participate in networking events to expand your social circle and hone your interpersonal skills."**

She finished with a thought-provoking statement, her voice filled with encouragement. **"Improving Emotional Intelligence is an ongoing journey that requires commitment and practice. By incorporating these strategies into our daily lives, we can cultivate greater self-awareness, self-regulation, empathy, and social skills, ultimately leading to more fulfilling relationships and success in both our personal and professional endeavors."**

The room filled with applause, the students clearly inspired and eager to apply what they had learned about enhancing their Emotional Intelligence. Dr. Marvis Carter smiled, knowing she had provided them with practical tools for their journey of emotional and intellectual growth.

4

Chapter 4: Comparing IQ and EQ

Key Differences Between IQ and EQ

The atmosphere in the lecture hall shifted as Dr. Marvis Carter began to explore the distinctions between Intellectual Intelligence (IQ) and Emotional Intelligence (EQ). She knew that understanding these differences was crucial for her students to appreciate the unique contributions of each form of intelligence to human cognition and behavior.

"**Good morning, everyone,**" Marvis greeted, her voice poised and confident. "**Today, we embark on a comparative journey between IQ and EQ. While both are forms of intelligence, they differ significantly in their nature, measurement, and impact on our lives.**"

She clicked the remote, and the screen displayed a side-by-side comparison of IQ and EQ. "**Let's start by examining the key differences between IQ and EQ,**" Marvis continued. "**While IQ measures cognitive abilities such as reasoning,** problem-solving, and memory, EQ focuses on understanding and managing emotions, both in oneself and others."

The next slide showcased examples of IQ test questions alongside scenarios requiring emotional intelligence. "**IQ tests typically involve tasks such as solving puzzles, analyzing patterns, and answering abstract questions,**" Marvis explained. "**In contrast, EQ assessments assess skills such as self-awareness, empathy, and social interaction through scenarios and self-report measures.**"

A hand went up in the front row. "**How do IQ and EQ differ in terms of measurement?**"

Marvis nodded, appreciating the question. "**Great question. IQ is typically measured using standardized tests that yield a numerical score, known as an intelligence quotient. These tests assess various cognitive abilities and provide a snapshot of an individual's intellectual capabilities.**"

She clicked to the next slide, which displayed a graph comparing IQ scores among individuals. "**EQ, on the other hand, is assessed using self-report questionnaires, performance-based tests, and 360-degree feedback,**" Marvis continued. "**These assessments provide insights into an individual's emotional skills, such as self-awareness, self-regulation, empathy, and social skills.**"

The screen transitioned to a chart displaying EQ scores and their implications. "**Unlike IQ, which remains relatively stable throughout adulthood, EQ is more malleable and can be developed over time,**" Marvis noted. "**Through intentional effort and practice, individuals can enhance their emotional intelligence and improve their ability to** navigate social and emotional challenges."

A short video clip played, featuring Dr. Daniel Goleman discussing the significance of EQ. "**Emotional Intelligence is the ability to recognize, understand, and manage our own emotions and the emotions of others,**" Goleman emphasized. "**It's not about being emotional but about being smart with emotions.**"

Marvis paused the video, letting Goleman's words resonate. "**Goleman's insights highlight the practical relevance of Emotional Intelligence in our daily lives,**" she said. "**While IQ may determine academic and professional success to some extent, EQ often plays a more significant role in personal relationships, leadership effectiveness, and overall well-being.**"

The next slide showcased examples of how IQ and EQ manifest in different scenarios, from academic achievement to workplace performance to interpersonal relationships. "**In summary, while IQ and EQ are distinct forms of intelligence, they complement each other in shaping human cognition and behavior,**" Marvis concluded. "**By understanding their differences and leveraging their respective strengths, we can unlock our full potential and lead more fulfilling lives.**"

She finished with a thought-provoking statement, her voice filled with encouragement. "**As we continue to explore the interplay between IQ and EQ, remember that both are valuable assets in our journey of growth and self-discovery. By cultivating both forms of intelligence, we can achieve a harmonious balance between intellect and emotion, leading to greater resilience, success, and happiness.**"

The room filled with applause, the students clearly inspired and eager to delve deeper into the nuanced relationship between IQ and EQ. Dr. Marvis Carter smiled, knowing she had ignited their curiosity and provided them with valuable insights for their intellectual exploration.

Strengths and Weaknesses of Each

The lecture hall buzzed with anticipation as Dr. Marvis Carter prepared to delve into the strengths and weaknesses of Intellectual Intelligence (IQ) and Emotional Intelligence (EQ). She knew that understanding these nuances would provide her students with a comprehensive perspective on the two forms of intelligence and their implications for personal and professional success.

"**Welcome back, everyone,**" Marvis began, her voice projecting warmth and authority. "**Now, let's explore the strengths and weaknesses of IQ and EQ, shedding light on the unique attributes of each form of intelligence.**"

She clicked the remote, and the screen displayed a comparison chart highlighting the strengths and weaknesses of IQ and EQ side by side. "**While IQ excels in measuring cognitive abilities such as logical reasoning, problem-solving, and analytical thinking,**" Marvis explained, "**its strength lies in predicting academic and professional success, particularly in traditional educational and occupational settings.**"

A hand rose in the front row. "**What are some examples of IQ's strengths in real-world applications?**"

Marvis nodded, acknowledging the question. "**Great question. In academic settings, individuals with high IQ scores often excel in standardized tests, perform well in** challenging courses, and demonstrate advanced problem-solving abilities," she replied. "**Similarly, in the workplace, employees with high IQs may excel in roles that require complex analysis, strategic planning, and innovation.**"

She clicked to the next slide, which highlighted the strengths of Emotional Intelligence. "**In contrast, Emotional Intelligence shines in areas such as self-awareness, empathy, social skills, and emotional regulation,**" Marvis continued. "**Its strength lies in fostering positive relationships, effective communication, and leadership effectiveness, leading to greater overall well-being and success in personal and professional domains.**"

The screen transitioned to examples of EQ's strengths in interpersonal relationships and leadership roles. "**Individuals with high EQ scores often excel in roles that require strong interpersonal skills, such as sales, customer service, and team leadership,**" Marvis noted. "**They can navigate social dynamics effectively, build rapport with others, and resolve conflicts constructively.**"

A short video clip played, featuring testimonials from individuals who had benefited from developing their Emotional Intelligence. "**Enhancing my EQ has transformed my personal and professional life,**" one individual shared. "**It's helped me communicate more effectively, manage stress, and build stronger relationships with my colleagues and clients.**"

Marvis paused the video, letting the testimonials resonate with the students. "**These testimonials illustrate the practical benefits of Emotional Intelligence in various aspects of life,**" she said. "**While IQ may open doors to academic and professional opportunities, EQ often determines how** well we navigate those opportunities and thrive in diverse social and emotional contexts."

The next slide showcased examples of the weaknesses of both IQ and EQ. "**Despite their strengths, both forms of intelligence have their limitations,**" Marvis explained. "**For example, individuals with high IQs may struggle in areas that require emotional insight and interpersonal skills, such as managing relationships, resolving conflicts, and understanding nonverbal cues.**"

A hand went up in the middle row. "**How about the weaknesses of EQ?**"

Marvis nodded, addressing the question. "**Good question. While Emotional Intelligence is vital for social and emotional well-being, individuals with high EQs may face challenges in highly analytical or technical fields where cognitive abilities are paramount,**" she replied. "**Additionally, an overemphasis on emotions without rational analysis can sometimes lead to impulsive decision-making or undue influence of subjective biases.**"

The final slide summarized the strengths and weaknesses of IQ and EQ, emphasizing the importance of balance between the two forms of intelligence. "**In summary, both IQ and EQ offer unique strengths and weaknesses that complement each other,**" Marvis concluded. "**By understanding and leveraging the strengths of each form of intelligence while addressing their respective weaknesses, we can achieve a harmonious balance that maximizes our potential for success and well-being.**"

She finished with a thought-provoking statement, her voice filled with encouragement. "**As we continue to explore the interplay between IQ and EQ, remember that both** are valuable assets in our journey of growth and self-discovery. By cultivating a balanced blend of intellect and emotion, we can navigate life's challenges with wisdom, resilience, and grace."

The room filled with applause, the students clearly inspired and eager to delve deeper into the complexities of IQ and EQ. Dr. Marvis Carter smiled, knowing she had provided them with valuable insights for their intellectual exploration.

Case Studies: High IQ vs. High EQ

The anticipation in the lecture hall heightened as Dr. Marvis Carter prepared to illustrate the differences between individuals with high Intellectual Intelligence (IQ) and those with high Emotional Intelligence (EQ) through compelling case studies. She knew that these real-life examples would bring the theoretical concepts to life, allowing her students to grasp the practical implications of IQ and EQ in diverse contexts.

"**Welcome back, everyone,**" Marvis greeted, her voice filled with enthusiasm. "**Today, we'll explore the contrasting experiences of individuals with high IQ and high EQ through insightful case studies. These stories will highlight the unique strengths and challenges associated with each form of intelligence.**"

She clicked the remote, and the screen displayed the first case study: Alex, a brilliant engineer with an exceptionally high IQ. "**Let's start with Alex,**" Marvis began. "**With an IQ in the genius range, Alex excelled academically from a young age. His exceptional problem-solving abilities and analytical skills propelled him to the top of his field, earning him prestigious awards and accolades.**"

The next slide showcased Alex receiving an award for his groundbreaking research in artificial intelligence. **"Despite his undeniable intellectual prowess, Alex struggled in interpersonal relationships,"** Marvis explained. **"His single-minded focus on his work often led to social isolation and difficulty connecting with others on a personal level. While his IQ opened doors to academic and professional success, his lack of emotional insight and social skills hindered his ability to build meaningful relationships outside of his field."**

A hand went up in the front row. **"How could Alex improve his social skills and emotional insight?"**

Marvis nodded, addressing the question. **"Great question. By developing his Emotional Intelligence through practices such as active listening, empathy-building exercises, and social interaction, Alex could enhance his ability to connect with others on a deeper level,"** she replied. **"While his IQ remains a valuable asset, integrating EQ into his interpersonal interactions could lead to greater overall well-being and fulfillment."**

She clicked to the next slide, which featured the second case study: Sarah, a compassionate nurse with a remarkable ability to connect with patients and colleagues. **"Now, let's turn to Sarah,"** Marvis continued. **"With a high level of Emotional Intelligence, Sarah excels in her role as a nurse, providing compassionate care and support to her patients during challenging times."**

The screen displayed Sarah comforting a patient with a reassuring smile. **"Sarah's empathy, compassion, and ability to read emotional cues enable her to establish trust and rapport with her patients,"** Marvis explained.

"Her high EQ not only enhances her effectiveness as a caregiver but also fosters a positive work environment where colleagues feel valued and supported."

A hand went up in the middle row. "**What challenges might Sarah face due to her high EQ?**"

Marvis considered the question thoughtfully. "**While Sarah's high EQ serves her well in her caregiving role, she may sometimes struggle with setting boundaries and managing her own emotions in emotionally charged situations,**" she replied. "**Additionally, her empathetic nature could lead to emotional exhaustion or burnout if not properly managed. Balancing empathy with self-care is essential for maintaining well-being in demanding professions.**"

The final slide summarized the key takeaways from the case studies, emphasizing the importance of a balanced blend of IQ and EQ. "**In summary, while individuals with high IQ may excel in analytical tasks and problem-solving, those with high EQ often thrive in interpersonal relationships and leadership roles,**" Marvis concluded. "**By understanding and leveraging the strengths of both forms of intelligence, we can achieve a harmonious balance that maximizes our potential for success and well-being.**"

She finished with a thought-provoking statement, her voice filled with encouragement. "**As we continue to explore the interplay between IQ and EQ, remember that both are valuable assets in our journey of growth and self-discovery. By cultivating a balanced blend of intellect and emotion, we can navigate life's challenges with wisdom, resilience, and grace.**"

The room filled with applause, the students clearly inspired and eager to delve deeper into the complexities of IQ and EQ through real-life examples. Dr. Marvis Carter smiled, knowing she had provided them with valuable insights for their intellectual exploration.

Misconceptions and Myths

The lecture hall buzzed with anticipation as Dr. Marvis Carter prepared to debunk common misconceptions and myths surrounding Intellectual Intelligence (IQ) and Emotional Intelligence (EQ). She knew that addressing these misconceptions would clarify misunderstandings and deepen her students' understanding of the complexities of IQ and EQ.

"**Good morning, everyone,**" Marvis greeted, her voice resonating with authority. "**Today, we'll unravel some of the misconceptions and myths surrounding IQ and EQ, shedding light on the truth behind these often misunderstood forms of intelligence.**"

She clicked the remote, and the screen displayed a list of common misconceptions about IQ and EQ. "**Let's start by addressing the misconception that IQ is the sole determinant of intelligence and success,**" Marvis began. "**While IQ is an important measure of cognitive abilities, it is not the only factor that influences an individual's intellectual capabilities or potential for achievement.**"

The next slide showcased examples of individuals with diverse talents and strengths beyond traditional measures of intelligence. "**Many successful individuals, such as artists, musicians, and entrepreneurs, demonstrate exceptional talents and abilities that may not be captured by IQ tests,**" Marvis explained. "**Creativity, emotional insight, and perseverance are just as important as cognitive abilities in determining one's overall intelligence and potential for success."

A hand went up in the front row. "**What are some other misconceptions about IQ?**"

Marvis nodded, acknowledging the question. "**Another common misconception is that IQ is fixed and unchangeable,**" she replied. "**While IQ scores may remain relatively stable over time, they can also be influenced by factors such as education, experience, and environmental enrichment. Additionally, individuals can enhance their cognitive abilities through learning, practice, and cognitive training.**"

She clicked to the next slide, which highlighted misconceptions about Emotional Intelligence. "**Now, let's turn our attention to EQ,**" Marvis continued. "**One common myth is that Emotional Intelligence is synonymous with being 'soft' or 'weak.' In reality, individuals with high EQ demonstrate strength, resilience, and adaptability in navigating complex emotional situations.**"

The screen transitioned to examples of leaders who exemplify strong Emotional Intelligence in their decision-making and interpersonal interactions. "**Leaders with high EQ are often more effective in inspiring and motivating their teams, managing conflicts, and fostering a positive work culture,**" Marvis noted. "**Their ability to understand and manage emotions enhances their leadership effectiveness and contributes to organizational success.**"

A hand went up in the middle row. "**What are some misconceptions about EQ in the workplace?**"

Marvis considered the question thoughtfully. "**One common misconception is that EQ is solely about being 'nice' or 'agreeable,'" she replied. "While empathy and interpersonal skills are important components of EQ, it also involves self-awareness, emotional regulation, and assertiveness. Individuals with high EQ can navigate challenging situations with confidence and integrity, while still maintaining healthy boundaries and advocating for their needs."

The final slide summarized the key takeaways from the discussion, emphasizing the importance of dispelling misconceptions and embracing the complexity of IQ and EQ. "**In summary, understanding the truth behind common misconceptions and myths surrounding IQ and EQ is essential for cultivating a balanced and nuanced perspective on intelligence,**" Marvis concluded. "**By recognizing the diverse talents and strengths that individuals possess, we can create environments that nurture and celebrate the full spectrum of human intelligence and potential.**"

She finished with a thought-provoking statement, her voice filled with encouragement. "**As we continue to explore the interplay between IQ and EQ, let's challenge ourselves to question assumptions, embrace diversity, and cultivate a deeper understanding of the multifaceted nature of intelligence.**"

The room filled with applause, the students clearly inspired and eager to apply their newfound insights to their studies and personal growth. Dr. Marvis Carter smiled, knowing she had empowered them to navigate the complexities of IQ and EQ with wisdom and clarity.

Integrating IQ and EQ for Balanced Intelligence

The lecture hall fell silent as Dr. Marvis Carter prepared to explore the concept of integrating Intellectual Intelligence (IQ) and Emotional Intelligence (EQ) for balanced intelligence. She knew that understanding how these two forms of intelligence intersect and complement each other was key to unlocking human potential and fostering holistic personal and professional development.

"**Welcome back, everyone,**" Marvis began, her voice carrying a sense of anticipation. "**Today, we'll delve into the power of integrating IQ and EQ to cultivate balanced intelligence—a synergistic blend of cognitive abilities and emotional insight that enables individuals to thrive in diverse contexts.**"

She clicked the remote, and the screen displayed a Venn diagram illustrating the intersection of IQ and EQ. "**Let's start by exploring how IQ and EQ can work together to enhance our cognitive and emotional capabilities,**" Marvis explained. "**While IQ focuses on cognitive abilities such as logical reasoning, problem-solving, and memory, EQ encompasses skills such as self-awareness, empathy, and social interaction.**"

The next slide showcased examples of how individuals can leverage their combined IQ and EQ to achieve success in various aspects of life. "**By integrating IQ and EQ, individuals can enhance their decision-making, communication, and leadership effectiveness,**" Marvis noted. "**For example, leaders with high IQs can benefit from developing their EQ to build stronger relationships with their team members, inspire trust and collaboration, and** navigate complex interpersonal dynamics with finesse."

A hand went up in the front row. "**How can we integrate IQ and EQ in our daily lives?**"

Marvis nodded, appreciating the question. "**Great question. One way to integrate IQ and EQ is through reflective practices such as journaling, meditation, and self-assessment,**" she replied. "**These practices foster self-awareness and emotional insight, allowing individuals to understand their cognitive strengths and weaknesses and how they impact their emotions and behaviors.**"

She clicked to the next slide, which highlighted strategies for developing a balanced blend of IQ and EQ. "**Another strategy is to seek feedback from others and engage in continuous learning and personal development,**" Marvis continued. "**By soliciting feedback from trusted mentors, colleagues, and friends, individuals can gain valuable insights into their blind spots and areas for growth, both cognitively and emotionally.**"

The screen transitioned to examples of organizations that prioritize both IQ and EQ in their talent development initiatives. "**In progressive organizations, leaders recognize the value of cultivating a diverse workforce with a balanced blend of cognitive and emotional capabilities,**" Marvis noted. "**They invest in training and development programs that enhance both IQ and EQ, fostering a culture of innovation, collaboration, and high performance.**"

A hand went up in the middle row. "**How can we foster a culture of balanced intelligence in our organizations?**"

Marvis considered the question thoughtfully. "**One way is to lead by example and promote a growth mindset that values continuous learning, feedback,** and self-improvement," she replied. "Encourage open communication, collaboration, and empathy among team members, and create opportunities for cross-functional collaboration and knowledge sharing."

The final slide summarized the key takeaways from the discussion, emphasizing the importance of integrating IQ and EQ for personal and organizational success. **"In summary, integrating IQ and EQ allows individuals to harness the full spectrum of their cognitive and emotional capabilities,"** Marvis concluded. **"By cultivating a balanced blend of intellect and emotion, we can navigate life's challenges with wisdom, resilience, and grace, ultimately leading to greater fulfillment and success."**

She finished with a thought-provoking statement, her voice filled with encouragement. **"As we continue to explore the interplay between IQ and EQ, let's embrace the power of balanced intelligence to create positive change in ourselves and the world around us."**

The room filled with applause, the students clearly inspired and eager to integrate IQ and EQ in their journey of personal and professional growth. Dr. Marvis Carter smiled, knowing she had empowered them with valuable insights for cultivating balanced intelligence in their lives.

5

Chapter 5: Emotional Intelligence in Leadership

The Role of EQ in Effective Leadership

The atmosphere in the lecture hall shifted as Dr. Marvis Carter prepared to explore the pivotal role of Emotional Intelligence (EQ) in effective leadership. She knew that understanding how EQ influences leadership effectiveness was crucial for her students' future success in managerial roles and beyond.

"**Good morning, everyone,**" Marvis greeted, her voice resonating with authority. "**Today, we embark on a journey to explore the transformative power of Emotional Intelligence in leadership. As we delve into the role of EQ, we'll uncover how it shapes the behaviors, decisions, and impact of effective leaders.**"

She clicked the remote, and the screen displayed a montage of iconic leaders from various fields, from business to politics to sports. "**Let's start by examining the role of EQ in** effective leadership," Marvis began. "**Leadership is not just about making decisions or giving orders; it's about inspiring, motivating, and empowering others to achieve common goals.**"

The next slide showcased examples of leaders who exemplify strong Emotional Intelligence in their leadership style. "**Leaders with high EQ demonstrate empathy, self-awareness, and social skills in their interactions with others,**" Marvis explained. "**They understand their own emotions and how they impact their behavior, as well as the emotions of those around them. This enables them to build trust, foster collaboration, and create a positive work environment.**"

A hand went up in the front row. "**How does EQ contribute to effective decision-making in leadership?**"

Marvis nodded, appreciating the question. "**Great question. EQ plays a crucial role in decision-making by helping leaders consider the emotions and perspectives of others,**" she replied. "**Leaders with high EQ are adept at listening to diverse viewpoints, managing conflicts constructively, and making decisions that balance the needs and interests of all stakeholders. This fosters buy-in, commitment, and alignment among team members, ultimately leading to more successful outcomes.**"

She clicked to the next slide, which highlighted the importance of empathy in leadership. "**Empathy is a cornerstone of effective leadership,**" Marvis continued. "**Leaders who demonstrate empathy understand the experiences, concerns, and aspirations of their team members. By showing genuine care and compassion, they build stronger relationships, inspire loyalty, and create a supportive** work culture where everyone feels valued and respected."

The screen transitioned to examples of leaders who prioritize empathy in their leadership approach. "**Empathetic leaders actively listen to their team members, validate their emotions, and offer support and encouragement,**" Marvis noted. "**They seek to understand the unique perspectives and needs of each individual, adapting their leadership style to meet them where they are. This cultivates a sense of belonging and psychological safety, enabling team members to thrive and contribute their best.**"

A hand went up in the middle row. "**How can leaders develop their Emotional Intelligence to become more effective?**"

Marvis considered the question thoughtfully. "**One way is through self-awareness and self-reflection,**" she replied. "**Leaders can take time to examine their own emotions, strengths, and areas for growth. They can also seek feedback from others and engage in leadership development programs that focus on enhancing EQ competencies such as self-regulation, empathy, and social skills.**"

The final slide summarized the key takeaways from the discussion, emphasizing the transformative impact of EQ on leadership effectiveness. "**In summary, Emotional Intelligence is a critical determinant of effective leadership,**" Marvis concluded. "**By cultivating empathy, self-awareness, and social skills, leaders can inspire, motivate, and empower their teams to achieve extraordinary results. In doing so, they not only drive organizational success but also create a lasting legacy of positive impact and growth.**"

She finished with a thought-provoking statement, her voice

filled with encouragement. **"As we continue to explore the interplay between EQ and leadership, let's challenge ourselves to embody the principles of Emotional Intelligence in our own leadership journeys, empowering ourselves and others to reach new heights of success and fulfillment."**

The room filled with applause, the students clearly inspired and eager to apply their newfound insights to their future leadership endeavors. Dr. Marvis Carter smiled, knowing she had provided them with valuable insights for their journey of leadership and personal growth.

Case Studies: Leaders with High EQ

The lecture hall brimmed with anticipation as Dr. Marvis Carter prepared to delve into real-life case studies of leaders who exemplify high Emotional Intelligence (EQ). She knew that these stories would illuminate the practical application of EQ principles in leadership and inspire her students to cultivate their own EQ competencies for success in their future roles.

"Welcome back, everyone," Marvis began, her voice carrying a sense of excitement. **"Today, we'll explore case studies of leaders who embody high Emotional Intelligence in their leadership style. Through these stories, we'll uncover the transformative impact of EQ on leadership effectiveness and organizational success."**

She clicked the remote, and the screen displayed the first case study: Anne, a CEO known for her empathetic leadership approach. **"Let's start with Anne,"** Marvis began. **"As the CEO of a multinational corporation, Anne leads with** empathy, compassion, and authenticity."

The next slide showcased Anne engaging with her team members, listening attentively to their ideas and concerns. **"Anne understands the importance of building strong relationships with her employees,"** Marvis explained. **"She takes time to connect with each team member on a personal level, showing genuine care and interest in their well-being."**

A hand went up in the front row. **"How does Anne's empathy contribute to her leadership effectiveness?"**

Marvis nodded, appreciating the question. **"Great question. Anne's empathy enables her to foster a culture of trust, collaboration, and innovation within her organization,"** she replied. **"By creating a supportive work environment where employees feel valued and respected, Anne inspires loyalty and commitment among her team members. This translates into higher morale, productivity, and retention rates, ultimately driving organizational success."**

She clicked to the next slide, which featured the second case study: John, a charismatic leader known for his emotional intelligence and adaptability. **"Now, let's turn to John,"** Marvis continued. **"As the head of a rapidly growing startup, John faces constant challenges and uncertainties. However, his high EQ enables him to navigate these challenges with resilience and grace."**

The screen displayed John addressing his team during a company-wide meeting, exuding confidence and optimism. **"John understands the importance of emotional resilience in leadership,"** Marvis noted. **"He remains calm under pressure, maintains a positive attitude in the face of adversity, and empowers his team to overcome obstacles** together."

A hand went up in the middle row. "**How does John's adaptability contribute to his leadership effectiveness?**"

Marvis considered the question thoughtfully. "**John's adaptability allows him to respond effectively to changing circumstances and seize opportunities for growth and innovation,**" she replied. "**He encourages experimentation, embraces failure as a learning opportunity, and fosters a culture of continuous improvement within his organization. This agility enables his team to stay ahead of the curve and thrive in a dynamic business environment.**"

The final slide summarized the key takeaways from the case studies, emphasizing the importance of empathy, resilience, and adaptability in effective leadership. "**In summary, leaders with high EQ demonstrate empathy, resilience, and adaptability in their interactions with others,**" Marvis concluded. "**By embodying these qualities, they inspire trust, foster collaboration, and drive organizational success. As aspiring leaders, let's draw inspiration from their examples and cultivate our own Emotional Intelligence for leadership excellence.**"

She finished with a thought-provoking statement, her voice filled with encouragement. "**As we continue to explore the interplay between EQ and leadership, let's challenge ourselves to learn from the experiences of these exemplary leaders and apply their insights to our own leadership journeys.**"

The room filled with applause, the students clearly inspired and eager to emulate the leadership qualities demonstrated in the case studies. Dr. Marvis Carter smiled, knowing she had provided them with valuable insights for their future leadership roles.

Developing Emotional Competence in Leaders

The lecture hall brimmed with anticipation as Dr. Marvis Carter prepared to explore strategies for developing Emotional Competence in leaders. She knew that equipping her students with practical tools and techniques for enhancing their Emotional Intelligence (EQ) would empower them to become effective leaders capable of inspiring and empowering others.

"**Good morning, everyone,**" Marvis greeted, her voice exuding warmth and enthusiasm. "**Today, we'll delve into the essential components of Emotional Competence and explore how leaders can cultivate their Emotional Intelligence for greater effectiveness and impact.**"

She clicked the remote, and the screen displayed a diagram outlining the components of Emotional Competence: self-awareness, self-regulation, empathy, social skills, and motivation. "**Let's start by examining the key components of Emotional Competence,**" Marvis began. "**Self-awareness involves understanding one's emotions, strengths, weaknesses, and values. Self-regulation entails managing one's emotions, impulses, and reactions effectively.**"

The next slide showcased examples of leaders demonstrating self-awareness and self-regulation in their leadership approach. "**Leaders who cultivate self-awareness and self-regulation are better equipped to make informed decisions, manage stress, and navigate complex interpersonal dynamics,**" Marvis explained. "**They take ownership of their emotions and behaviors, leading by example and inspiring others** to do the same."

A hand went up in the front row. "**How can leaders develop their self-awareness and self-regulation?**"

Marvis nodded, appreciating the question. "**Great question. One way is through practices such as mindfulness, reflection, and journaling,**" she replied. "**These practices help leaders tune into their thoughts, emotions, and reactions, fostering greater self-awareness and self-understanding. Additionally, seeking feedback from others and engaging in leadership development programs can provide valuable insights into areas for growth and improvement.**"

She clicked to the next slide, which highlighted the importance of empathy and social skills in leadership. "**Empathy involves understanding and empathizing with the emotions and perspectives of others,**" Marvis continued. "**Leaders who demonstrate empathy create a culture of trust, collaboration, and inclusivity within their teams.**"

The screen transitioned to examples of leaders who prioritize empathy and social skills in their leadership style. "**Leaders who excel in social skills are adept at building rapport, communicating effectively, and resolving conflicts,**" Marvis noted. "**They foster open dialogue, encourage diverse viewpoints, and empower their team members to contribute their best.**"

A hand went up in the middle row. "**How can leaders develop their empathy and social skills?**"

Marvis considered the question thoughtfully. "**One approach is to practice active listening and perspective-taking,**" she replied. "**Leaders can seek to understand the experiences and viewpoints of their team members, validate their emotions, and communicate with empathy** and authenticity. Additionally, participating in team-building activities, communication workshops, and leadership training programs can enhance social skills and interpersonal effectiveness."

The final slide summarized the key takeaways from the discussion, emphasizing the importance of developing Emotional Competence for effective leadership. "**In summary, cultivating Emotional Competence enables leaders to inspire, motivate, and empower their teams to achieve extraordinary results,**" Marvis concluded. "**By developing self-awareness, self-regulation, empathy, and social skills, leaders can create a culture of trust, collaboration, and innovation that drives organizational success and fosters personal growth.**"

She finished with a thought-provoking statement, her voice filled with encouragement. "**As we continue to explore the interplay between EQ and leadership, let's challenge ourselves to cultivate our Emotional Competence and unleash our full potential as leaders.**"

The room filled with applause, the students clearly inspired and eager to apply the strategies for developing Emotional Competence in their own leadership journeys. Dr. Marvis Carter smiled, knowing she had provided them with valuable insights for their future success as leaders.

Empathy and Influence: Tools for Leaders

The atmosphere in the lecture hall shifted as Dr. Marvis Carter prepared to explore empathy and influence as essential tools for leaders. She knew that understanding how empathy shapes influence would empower her students to build stronger

CHAPTER 5: EMOTIONAL INTELLIGENCE IN LEADERSHIP

relationships, foster collaboration, and drive positive change in their organizations and communities.

"**Welcome back, everyone,**" Marvis began, her voice radiating warmth and authority. "**Today, we'll explore empathy and influence as powerful tools for effective leadership. By understanding how empathy drives influence, we can unlock new possibilities for creating impact and inspiring others.**"

She clicked the remote, and the screen displayed a quote: *"Empathy is the ability to understand and share the feelings of others."* "**Let's start by examining the role of empathy in leadership,**" Marvis continued. "**Empathy enables leaders to connect with others on a deeper level, understand their perspectives, and respond with compassion and understanding.**"

The next slide showcased examples of leaders who exemplify empathy in their leadership approach. "**Leaders who demonstrate empathy create a culture of trust, collaboration, and inclusivity within their teams,**" Marvis explained. "**They listen actively, validate the emotions of others, and show genuine care and concern for their well-being.**"

A hand went up in the front row. "**How does empathy contribute to a leader's influence?**"

Marvis nodded, appreciating the question. "**Great question. Empathy enhances a leader's ability to influence others by fostering trust, credibility, and rapport,**" she replied. "**When individuals feel understood and valued, they are more likely to listen to and be influenced by their leader's vision, goals, and ideas. Empathetic leaders inspire loyalty, commitment, and engagement among their team members, driving positive outcomes and organizational** success."

She clicked to the next slide, which highlighted examples of influential leaders who leverage empathy to drive change. **"Leaders who lead with empathy are able to inspire and mobilize others to action,"** Marvis noted. **"By understanding the needs and motivations of their stakeholders, they can tailor their messages and strategies to resonate with their audience, building consensus and generating support for their initiatives."**

The screen transitioned to examples of leaders who used empathy to navigate challenging situations and foster collaboration. **"Empathetic leaders are adept at resolving conflicts, building bridges across diverse perspectives, and finding win-win solutions that benefit all parties,"** Marvis explained. **"Their ability to understand and empathize with the emotions and perspectives of others enables them to build strong relationships and create a sense of shared purpose and unity."**

A hand went up in the middle row. **"How can leaders develop their empathy and use it to influence others positively?"**

Marvis considered the question thoughtfully. **"One approach is to practice active listening, empathy-building exercises, and perspective-taking,"** she replied. **"Leaders can strive to understand the experiences, emotions, and perspectives of their team members, stakeholders, and communities. By demonstrating genuine care and concern, they can build trust and rapport, laying the foundation for effective influence and collaboration."**

The final slide summarized the key takeaways from the discussion, emphasizing the transformative power of empathy in leadership. **"In summary, empathy is a fundamental tool for leaders seeking to influence positive change and drive organizational success,"** Marvis concluded. **"By cultivating empathy and using it to connect with others authentically, leaders can inspire trust, foster collaboration, and create a culture of empathy and inclusivity that transforms lives and organizations."**

She finished with a thought-provoking statement, her voice filled with encouragement. **"As we continue to explore the interplay between empathy and influence, let's challenge ourselves to lead with empathy and harness its transformative power to create a brighter, more compassionate world."**

The room filled with applause, the students clearly inspired and eager to apply the principles of empathy and influence in their own leadership endeavors. Dr. Marvis Carter smiled, knowing she had equipped them with valuable tools for making a positive difference in their organizations and communities.

Conflict Resolution and EQ

The anticipation in the lecture hall heightened as Dr. Marvis Carter prepared to delve into the relationship between Conflict Resolution and Emotional Intelligence (EQ). She knew that understanding how EQ influences conflict resolution would equip her students with invaluable skills for navigating interpersonal challenges and fostering harmony within their teams and organizations.

"Good morning, everyone," Marvis began, her voice filled with warmth and assurance. **"Today, we'll explore the criti-**

cal role of Emotional Intelligence in conflict resolution. By understanding how EQ influences our approach to conflict, we can transform challenges into opportunities for growth and collaboration."

She clicked the remote, and the screen displayed a quote: *"In the midst of conflict, lies opportunity."* "**Let's start by examining the connection between Emotional Intelligence and conflict resolution,**" Marvis continued. "**Emotional Intelligence equips leaders with the self-awareness, empathy, and communication skills needed to navigate conflicts effectively.**"

The next slide showcased examples of leaders who demonstrate EQ in their approach to conflict resolution. "**Leaders who excel in conflict resolution are able to remain calm under pressure, listen actively to all perspectives, and find win-win solutions that address the underlying needs and interests of all parties,**" Marvis explained. "**They approach conflicts with empathy, seeking to understand the emotions and motivations driving the disagreement.**"

A hand went up in the front row. "**How does Emotional Intelligence contribute to successful conflict resolution?**"

Marvis nodded, appreciating the question. "**Great question. Emotional Intelligence enables leaders to manage their own emotions and reactions, as well as those of others, during conflicts,**" she replied. "**By staying grounded and composed, leaders can de-escalate tensions, foster open communication, and create a safe space for constructive dialogue and problem-solving.**"

She clicked to the next slide, which highlighted examples of leaders who leverage EQ to resolve conflicts and build stronger relationships. "**Leaders who prioritize Emotional**

Intelligence in conflict resolution are able to transform conflicts into opportunities for growth and collaboration," Marvis noted. "By addressing underlying emotions and concerns, they can uncover common ground, build trust, and strengthen relationships within their teams."

The screen transitioned to examples of leaders who use EQ to navigate challenging interpersonal dynamics and build consensus. "Emotionally intelligent leaders are adept at facilitating difficult conversations, managing conflicts constructively, and finding creative solutions that satisfy the needs and interests of all parties involved," Marvis explained. "Their ability to foster empathy, trust, and mutual respect enables them to resolve conflicts in a way that strengthens rather than undermines team cohesion and productivity."

A hand went up in the middle row. "How can leaders develop their Emotional Intelligence to become more effective in conflict resolution?"

Marvis considered the question thoughtfully. "One approach is to practice self-awareness and self-regulation," she replied. "Leaders can reflect on their own triggers, biases, and emotional responses during conflicts, and learn to manage them effectively. Additionally, developing empathy and active listening skills can help leaders understand the perspectives and emotions of others, facilitating more empathetic and collaborative conflict resolution."

The final slide summarized the key takeaways from the discussion, emphasizing the importance of Emotional Intelligence in transforming conflicts into opportunities for growth and collaboration. "In summary, Emotional Intelligence equips leaders with the skills and mindset needed to navigate conflicts effectively," Marvis concluded. "**By fostering self-awareness, empathy, and communication skills, leaders can resolve conflicts in a way that strengthens relationships, builds trust, and fosters a culture of collaboration and innovation.**"

She finished with a thought-provoking statement, her voice filled with encouragement. "**As we continue to explore the interplay between EQ and conflict resolution, let's challenge ourselves to embrace conflicts as opportunities for learning, growth, and relationship-building. By cultivating our Emotional Intelligence, we can transform conflicts into catalysts for positive change and collective success.**"

The room filled with applause, the students clearly inspired and eager to apply the principles of Emotional Intelligence to their approach to conflict resolution. Dr. Marvis Carter smiled, knowing she had empowered them with invaluable skills for fostering harmony and collaboration in their future leadership roles.

Leading with Heart: Transformational Leadership

The anticipation in the lecture hall reached its peak as Dr. Marvis Carter prepared to explore the concept of leading with heart and its connection to transformational leadership. She knew that discussing the profound impact of Emotional Intelligence (EQ) on leadership effectiveness would inspire her students to cultivate empathy, authenticity, and vision in their own leadership journeys.

"**Welcome back, everyone,**" Marvis began, her voice filled with passion and conviction. **"Today, we embark on a journey to explore the transformative power of leading with heart—the essence of transformational leadership. By understanding how Emotional Intelligence shapes our ability to lead with authenticity, empathy, and vision, we can inspire positive change and create lasting impact."**

She clicked the remote, and the screen displayed a quote: *"Leadership is not about being in charge. It's about taking care of those in your charge."* **"Let's start by examining the essence of leading with heart,"** Marvis continued. **"Leading with heart means leading with authenticity, empathy, and integrity. It's about connecting with others on a deeper level, inspiring them to reach their full potential, and fostering a sense of purpose and belonging within the organization."**

The next slide showcased examples of leaders who embody transformational leadership principles in their leadership approach. **"Transformational leaders inspire and empower others to achieve extraordinary results,"** Marvis explained. **"They lead by example, demonstrating a strong moral compass, a clear sense of purpose, and a genuine concern for the well-being of their team members."**

A hand went up in the front row. **"How does leading with heart contribute to transformational leadership?"**

Marvis nodded, appreciating the question. **"Great question. Leading with heart fosters trust, loyalty, and commitment among team members,"** she replied. **"When leaders demonstrate empathy, authenticity, and integrity, they create a culture of psychological safety and empowerment where individuals feel valued, respected, and motivated to contribute their best."**

She clicked to the next slide, which highlighted examples of transformational leaders who use Emotional Intelligence to inspire and mobilize their teams. "**Transformational leaders leverage Emotional Intelligence to connect with others on an emotional level,**" Marvis noted. "**They communicate their vision with passion and conviction, inspire others to share in that vision, and empower them to take ownership of their roles in achieving it.**"

The screen transitioned to examples of leaders who prioritize the development and growth of their team members. "**Transformational leaders invest in the personal and professional development of their team members,**" Marvis explained. "**They provide mentorship, coaching, and opportunities for growth, enabling individuals to unlock their full potential and contribute meaningfully to the organization's success.**"

A hand went up in the middle row. "**How can leaders cultivate transformational leadership qualities in themselves?**"

Marvis considered the question thoughtfully. "**One approach is to lead by example and embody the values and principles of transformational leadership,**" she replied. "**Leaders can cultivate self-awareness, empathy, and authenticity, and strive to inspire and empower others through their actions and words. Additionally, seeking feedback, engaging in leadership development programs, and surrounding themselves with mentors and role models can help leaders continue to grow and evolve as transformational leaders.**"

The final slide summarized the key takeaways from the discussion, emphasizing the transformative impact of leading with heart on organizational culture and performance. **"In summary, leading with heart is the essence of transformational leadership,"** Marvis concluded. **"By cultivating Emotional Intelligence, authenticity, and vision, leaders can inspire positive change, foster a culture of trust and collaboration, and empower their teams to achieve extraordinary results."**

She finished with a thought-provoking statement, her voice filled with encouragement. **"As we continue to explore the interplay between EQ and transformational leadership, let's challenge ourselves to lead with heart and create a brighter, more compassionate future for ourselves and those we lead."**

The room filled with applause, the students clearly inspired and eager to embrace the principles of leading with heart in their own leadership journeys. Dr. Marvis Carter smiled, knowing she had ignited a spark of transformation in her students' hearts and minds.

6

Chapter 6: Intellectual Intelligence in Problem Solving

Analytical Thinking and IQ

The energy in the lecture hall surged as Dr. Marvis Carter prepared to delve into the intricate relationship between Intellectual Intelligence (IQ) and analytical thinking in problem-solving. She knew that exploring how IQ influences analytical thinking would provide her students with valuable insights into approaching complex challenges with clarity, precision, and creativity.

"**Good morning, everyone,**" Marvis began, her voice resonating with enthusiasm and curiosity. "**Today, we embark on a journey to explore the role of Intellectual Intelligence in problem-solving, with a focus on analytical thinking and IQ. By understanding how IQ influences our ability to analyze information, identify patterns, and generate innovative solutions, we can unlock new possibilities for tackling the toughest of challenges.**"

CHAPTER 6: INTELLECTUAL INTELLIGENCE IN PROBLEM SOLVING

She clicked the remote, and the screen displayed a quote: *"In the midst of complexity, lies simplicity."* **"Let's start by examining the essence of analytical thinking and its connection to IQ,"** Marvis continued. **"Analytical thinking involves breaking down complex problems into manageable components, identifying patterns and trends, and applying logical reasoning to arrive at sound conclusions."**

The next slide showcased examples of individuals who excel in analytical thinking due to their high IQ. **"Individuals with high IQs often demonstrate exceptional analytical thinking skills,"** Marvis explained. **"They have a keen ability to analyze data, recognize relationships between variables, and synthesize information from multiple sources to form a comprehensive understanding of the problem at hand."**

A hand went up in the front row. **"How does IQ contribute to analytical thinking and problem-solving?"**

Marvis nodded, appreciating the question. **"Great question. IQ influences analytical thinking by providing individuals with the cognitive abilities needed to process information efficiently and accurately,"** she replied. **"Individuals with higher IQs tend to have stronger working memory, faster processing speed, and superior problem-solving abilities, enabling them to approach complex problems with clarity, precision, and creativity."**

She clicked to the next slide, which highlighted examples of problem-solving scenarios where analytical thinking and high IQ play a crucial role. **"In real-world problem-solving scenarios, individuals with high IQs often excel in tasks that require logical reasoning, critical thinking, and decision-making,"** Marvis noted. **"They are adept at identifying** patterns, recognizing cause-and-effect relationships, and generating innovative solutions to address challenges effectively."

The screen transitioned to examples of groundbreaking discoveries and innovations driven by individuals with high IQs and exceptional analytical thinking skills. "**From scientific breakthroughs to technological advancements, individuals with high IQs have played a pivotal role in pushing the boundaries of human knowledge and innovation,**" Marvis explained. "**Their ability to think analytically and solve complex problems has led to transformative changes in fields ranging from medicine and engineering to finance and beyond.**"

A hand went up in the middle row. "**How can individuals develop their analytical thinking skills and leverage their IQ for problem-solving?**"

Marvis considered the question thoughtfully. "**One approach is to practice critical thinking exercises, puzzles, and logic games that challenge the mind and stimulate analytical thinking,**" she replied. "**Additionally, engaging in interdisciplinary learning, seeking feedback, and collaborating with others can help individuals broaden their perspectives and approach problem-solving from different angles, leading to more innovative and effective solutions.**"

The final slide summarized the key takeaways from the discussion, emphasizing the crucial role of analytical thinking and IQ in problem-solving. "**In summary, analytical thinking and high IQ are powerful assets in problem-solving,**" Marvis concluded. "**By honing their analytical thinking skills and leveraging their IQ, individuals can** approach complex challenges with confidence, creativity, and precision, leading to breakthrough discoveries and innovative solutions."

She finished with a thought-provoking statement, her voice filled with encouragement. **"As we continue to explore the interplay between IQ and problem-solving, let's challenge ourselves to cultivate our analytical thinking skills and unlock our full potential for solving the world's most pressing challenges."**

The room filled with applause, the students clearly inspired and eager to apply the principles of analytical thinking and IQ in their own problem-solving endeavors. Dr. Marvis Carter smiled, knowing she had equipped them with valuable tools for navigating the complexities of the world with clarity and ingenuity.

Creative Problem Solving

The lecture hall buzzed with anticipation as Dr. Marvis Carter prepared to explore the realm of creative problem-solving within the context of Intellectual Intelligence (IQ). She knew that discussing how IQ influences creative thinking would inspire her students to approach challenges with innovation, flexibility, and imagination.

"Welcome back, everyone," Marvis began, her voice filled with excitement and curiosity. **"Today, we'll embark on a journey to explore the intersection of Intellectual Intelligence and creative problem-solving. By understanding how IQ influences our ability to think outside the box, generate novel ideas, and find innovative solutions, we can unlock new pathways to addressing complex chal-**

lenges."

She clicked the remote, and the screen displayed a quote: *"Creativity is intelligence having fun."* **"Let's start by examining the essence of creative problem-solving and its connection to IQ,"** Marvis continued. **"Creative problem-solving involves thinking innovatively, generating original ideas, and approaching challenges from unconventional angles."**

The next slide showcased examples of individuals who excel in creative problem-solving due to their high IQ and imaginative thinking. **"Individuals with high IQs often demonstrate exceptional creativity in problem-solving,"** Marvis explained. **"They have the cognitive flexibility and mental agility needed to break free from conventional thinking patterns and explore unconventional solutions to complex problems."**

A hand went up in the front row. **"How does IQ contribute to creative problem-solving?"**

Marvis nodded, appreciating the question. **"Great question. IQ influences creative problem-solving by providing individuals with the cognitive resources and mental flexibility needed to think innovatively,"** she replied. **"Individuals with higher IQs tend to have stronger associative thinking skills, greater cognitive fluency, and superior divergent thinking abilities, enabling them to generate a wide range of ideas and explore multiple solution paths."**

She clicked to the next slide, which highlighted examples of problem-solving scenarios where creativity and high IQ play a crucial role. **"In real-world problem-solving scenarios, individuals with high IQs often excel in tasks that require creative thinking and innovation,"** Marvis noted. **"They are adept at reframing problems, connecting seemingly** unrelated concepts, and envisioning unconventional solutions that challenge the status quo."

The screen transitioned to examples of groundbreaking inventions and discoveries driven by individuals with high IQs and creative problem-solving skills. "**From revolutionary inventions to groundbreaking scientific discoveries, individuals with high IQs have played a pivotal role in pushing the boundaries of human knowledge and innovation,**" Marvis explained. "**Their ability to think creatively and solve complex problems has led to transformative changes in fields ranging from technology and art to science and beyond.**"

A hand went up in the middle row. "**How can individuals develop their creative problem-solving skills and leverage their IQ for innovation?**"

Marvis considered the question thoughtfully. "**One approach is to cultivate a growth mindset and embrace failure as a learning opportunity,**" she replied. "**By fostering a culture of experimentation, curiosity, and openness to new ideas, individuals can stimulate their creativity and explore innovative solutions to complex challenges. Additionally, engaging in activities such as brainstorming, mind mapping, and lateral thinking exercises can help individuals expand their creative thinking repertoire and unlock new pathways to innovation.**"

The final slide summarized the key takeaways from the discussion, emphasizing the crucial role of creative problem-solving and IQ in driving innovation. "**In summary, creative problem-solving and high IQ are powerful drivers of innovation and progress,**" Marvis concluded. "**By harnessing their creative potential and leveraging their IQ, individu-**

als can approach challenges with imagination, ingenuity, and insight, leading to breakthrough discoveries and transformative solutions."

She finished with a thought-provoking statement, her voice filled with encouragement. **"As we continue to explore the interplay between IQ and creative problem-solving, let's challenge ourselves to unleash our creative potential and embrace the power of innovation to shape a brighter future for ourselves and generations to come."**

The room filled with applause, the students clearly inspired and eager to apply the principles of creative problem-solving and IQ in their own endeavors. Dr. Marvis Carter smiled, knowing she had ignited a spark of creativity and innovation in her students' minds.

The Role of IQ in Strategic Planning

The lecture hall hummed with anticipation as Dr. Marvis Carter delved into the pivotal role of Intellectual Intelligence (IQ) in strategic planning. She knew that discussing how IQ influences strategic thinking would equip her students with the tools to develop comprehensive, forward-thinking strategies to navigate the complexities of today's world.

"Good morning, everyone," Marvis greeted, her voice imbued with enthusiasm and purpose. **"Today, we embark on a journey to explore the critical role of Intellectual Intelligence in strategic planning. By understanding how IQ shapes our ability to analyze data, anticipate trends, and formulate long-term strategies, we can pave the way for organizational success and resilience in an ever-changing landscape."**

She clicked the remote, and the screen displayed a quote: *"Strategy is the art of making choices."* **"Let's begin by examining the essence of strategic planning and its connection to IQ,"** Marvis continued. **"Strategic planning involves setting goals, identifying opportunities and threats, and developing action plans to achieve desired outcomes."**

The next slide showcased examples of individuals who excel in strategic planning due to their high IQ and analytical prowess. **"Individuals with high IQs often demonstrate exceptional strategic thinking skills,"** Marvis explained. **"They possess the cognitive abilities needed to analyze complex information, identify patterns, and make informed decisions that shape the direction and future of organizations."**

A hand went up in the front row. **"How does IQ contribute to strategic planning?"**

Marvis nodded, acknowledging the question. **"Excellent question. IQ influences strategic planning by providing individuals with the cognitive capacity to process information effectively and make sound decisions,"** she replied. **"Individuals with higher IQs tend to have stronger analytical skills, critical thinking abilities, and problem-solving prowess, enabling them to assess situations objectively, anticipate future trends, and formulate strategic plans that maximize opportunities and mitigate risks."**

She clicked to the next slide, which highlighted examples of strategic planning scenarios where high IQ plays a crucial role. **"In real-world strategic planning, individuals with high IQs often excel in tasks that require synthesizing vast amounts of data, identifying emerging trends, and developing innovative strategies to achieve organizational** goals," Marvis noted. "**They are adept at analyzing market dynamics, assessing competitive landscapes, and making strategic decisions that drive sustainable growth and competitive advantage.**"

The screen transitioned to examples of successful organizations led by individuals with high IQs and strategic acumen. "**From visionary entrepreneurs to corporate leaders, individuals with high IQs have played a pivotal role in shaping the strategic direction and success of organizations across industries,**" Marvis explained. "**Their ability to think strategically and make informed decisions has enabled them to navigate complex challenges, capitalize on emerging opportunities, and achieve long-term prosperity.**"

A hand went up in the middle row. "**How can individuals develop their strategic planning skills and leverage their IQ for success?**"

Marvis considered the question thoughtfully. "**One approach is to engage in strategic thinking exercises, scenario planning, and decision-making simulations that challenge the mind and stimulate strategic thinking,**" she replied. "**Additionally, seeking mentorship, studying successful strategic leaders, and staying informed about industry trends and market dynamics can help individuals hone their strategic planning skills and leverage their IQ to make informed decisions that drive organizational success.**"

The final slide summarized the key takeaways from the discussion, emphasizing the indispensable role of IQ in strategic planning. "**In summary, Intellectual Intelligence is a cornerstone of effective strategic planning,**" Marvis concluded. "**By harnessing their cognitive abilities and leveraging their IQ, individuals can develop comprehensive, forward-thinking strategies that position their organizations for success and resilience in an increasingly complex and competitive world.**"

She finished with a thought-provoking statement, her voice resonating with conviction. "**As we continue to explore the interplay between IQ and strategic planning, let's challenge ourselves to think strategically, make informed decisions, and shape the future with wisdom and foresight.**"

The room filled with applause, the students clearly inspired and eager to apply the principles of strategic planning and IQ in their own endeavors. Dr. Marvis Carter smiled, knowing she had equipped them with invaluable tools for navigating the complexities of the modern world with clarity and purpose.

Critical Thinking Skills

The lecture hall crackled with anticipation as Dr. Marvis Carter delved into the critical importance of critical thinking skills within the realm of Intellectual Intelligence (IQ). She knew that exploring how IQ influences critical thinking would empower her students to dissect information, evaluate arguments, and make informed decisions with clarity and precision.

"**Welcome back, everyone,**" Marvis greeted, her voice brimming with energy and enthusiasm. "**Today, we'll embark on a journey to explore the indispensable role of critical thinking skills in problem-solving and decision-making. By understanding how IQ shapes our ability to analyze** information, question assumptions, and form reasoned judgments, we can navigate the complexities of our world with confidence and insight."

She clicked the remote, and the screen displayed a quote: *"In a world of information overload, critical thinking is a survival skill."* "Let's begin by examining the essence of critical thinking and its connection to IQ," Marvis continued. "Critical thinking involves actively and skillfully analyzing information, questioning assumptions, and evaluating evidence to guide belief and action."

The next slide showcased examples of individuals who excel in critical thinking due to their high IQ and analytical prowess. "Individuals with high IQs often demonstrate exceptional critical thinking skills," Marvis explained. "They possess the cognitive abilities needed to approach problems with logic, objectivity, and skepticism, enabling them to sift through vast amounts of information and discern patterns, inconsistencies, and underlying truths."

A hand went up in the front row. "How does IQ contribute to critical thinking?"

Marvis nodded, acknowledging the question. "Excellent question. IQ influences critical thinking by providing individuals with the cognitive capacity to process information effectively and make sound judgments," she replied. "Individuals with higher IQs tend to have stronger analytical skills, logical reasoning abilities, and problem-solving acumen, enabling them to evaluate arguments, detect fallacies, and arrive at well-reasoned conclusions."

She clicked to the next slide, which highlighted examples of critical thinking scenarios where high IQ plays a crucial role. "In real-world situations, individuals with high

IQs often excel in tasks that require analyzing complex information, weighing competing arguments, and making informed decisions," Marvis noted. "They are adept at identifying biases, assessing the credibility of sources, and synthesizing diverse perspectives to arrive at balanced and nuanced judgments."

The screen transitioned to examples of successful individuals and organizations led by individuals with high IQs and robust critical thinking skills. "**From pioneering scientists to astute business leaders, individuals with high IQs have harnessed the power of critical thinking to drive innovation, solve problems, and achieve success,**" Marvis explained. "Their ability to think critically and make informed decisions has enabled them to navigate challenges, capitalize on opportunities, and contribute meaningfully to their fields."

A hand went up in the middle row. "**How can individuals develop their critical thinking skills and leverage their IQ for success?**"

Marvis considered the question thoughtfully. "**One approach is to engage in exercises that challenge assumptions, evaluate arguments, and analyze evidence,**" she replied. "Additionally, seeking diverse perspectives, soliciting feedback, and practicing intellectual humility can help individuals cultivate a robust critical thinking mindset and leverage their IQ to make well-informed decisions that drive success."

The final slide summarized the key takeaways from the discussion, emphasizing the indispensable role of IQ in critical thinking. "**In summary, Intellectual Intelligence is a catalyst for effective critical thinking,**" Marvis concluded. **"By harnessing their cognitive abilities and honing their critical thinking skills, individuals can navigate the complexities of our world with clarity, objectivity, and discernment, empowering them to make informed decisions that lead to success and fulfillment."**

She finished with a thought-provoking statement, her voice resonating with conviction. **"As we continue to explore the interplay between IQ and critical thinking, let's challenge ourselves to cultivate a robust critical thinking mindset and embrace the power of reason and evidence to guide our beliefs and actions."**

The room filled with applause, the students clearly inspired and eager to apply the principles of critical thinking and IQ in their own endeavors. Dr. Marvis Carter smiled, knowing she had equipped them with invaluable tools for navigating the complexities of the modern world with clarity and insight.

Enhancing Cognitive Abilities

The lecture hall brimmed with anticipation as Dr. Marvis Carter delved into the fascinating realm of enhancing cognitive abilities within the context of Intellectual Intelligence (IQ). She knew that exploring how IQ influences cognitive enhancement would empower her students to optimize their mental faculties, boost their productivity, and achieve their fullest potential.

"Welcome back, everyone," Marvis greeted, her voice pulsating with enthusiasm and purpose. **"Today, we embark on a journey to explore the exciting possibilities of enhancing cognitive abilities through the lens of Intellectual Intelligence. By understanding how IQ shapes our cognitive functions and exploring strategies for cognitive**

enhancement, we can unlock new pathways to personal and professional growth."

She clicked the remote, and the screen displayed a quote: *"The mind is not a vessel to be filled, but a fire to be kindled."* **"Let's begin by examining the essence of cognitive enhancement and its connection to IQ,"** Marvis continued. **"Cognitive enhancement involves the use of various techniques and strategies to optimize cognitive functions such as memory, attention, and problem-solving."**

The next slide showcased examples of individuals who excel in cognitive enhancement due to their high IQ and proactive approach to mental fitness. **"Individuals with high IQs often demonstrate exceptional cognitive abilities,"** Marvis explained. **"They are proactive in seeking ways to optimize their mental faculties, whether through lifestyle modifications, cognitive training exercises, or neuroenhancement techniques."**

A hand went up in the front row. **"How does IQ contribute to cognitive enhancement?"**

Marvis nodded, acknowledging the question. **"Excellent question. IQ influences cognitive enhancement by providing individuals with a strong foundation of cognitive abilities,"** she replied. **"Individuals with higher IQs tend to have greater neuroplasticity, faster information processing speed, and superior working memory capacity, making them more receptive to cognitive enhancement interventions and more likely to experience positive outcomes."**

She clicked to the next slide, which highlighted examples of cognitive enhancement strategies where high IQ plays a crucial role. **"In real-world scenarios, individuals with** high IQs often excel in tasks that require sustained attention, mental agility, and creative problem-solving," Marvis noted. "**They are adept at leveraging cognitive enhancement techniques such as mindfulness meditation, brain training games, and nutritional interventions to optimize their cognitive performance and achieve their goals.**"

The screen transitioned to examples of successful individuals and organizations led by individuals with high IQs and enhanced cognitive abilities. "**From innovative entrepreneurs to visionary leaders, individuals with high IQs have leveraged cognitive enhancement to fuel their success and drive positive change,**" Marvis explained. "**Their commitment to optimizing their cognitive abilities has enabled them to stay sharp, focused, and adaptive in an increasingly complex and fast-paced world.**"

A hand went up in the middle row. "**How can individuals enhance their cognitive abilities and leverage their IQ for success?**"

Marvis considered the question thoughtfully. "**One approach is to adopt a holistic approach to cognitive enhancement, incorporating strategies such as regular exercise, healthy nutrition, quality sleep, and mental stimulation into their daily routines,**" she replied. "**Additionally, engaging in cognitive training exercises, seeking professional guidance, and staying curious and intellectually engaged can help individuals maximize their cognitive potential and leverage their IQ for success.**"

The final slide summarized the key takeaways from the discussion, emphasizing the transformative potential of cognitive enhancement. "**In summary, Intellectual Intelligence** lays the groundwork for cognitive enhancement," Marvis concluded. **"By embracing a proactive approach to mental fitness and leveraging cognitive enhancement strategies, individuals can optimize their cognitive abilities, boost their productivity, and achieve their fullest potential in all areas of life."**

She finished with a thought-provoking statement, her voice resonating with conviction. **"As we continue to explore the interplay between IQ and cognitive enhancement, let's challenge ourselves to cultivate a growth mindset and embrace the endless possibilities of the human mind."**

The room filled with applause, the students clearly inspired and eager to apply the principles of cognitive enhancement and IQ in their own endeavors. Dr. Marvis Carter smiled, knowing she had ignited a spark of curiosity and ambition in her students' hearts and minds.

Problem-Solving Techniques: Best Practices

The anticipation in the lecture hall reached its peak as Dr. Marvis Carter delved into the realm of problem-solving techniques within the context of Intellectual Intelligence (IQ). She knew that exploring effective problem-solving strategies would equip her students with the tools to tackle challenges with confidence, creativity, and precision.

"Good morning, everyone," Marvis greeted, her voice filled with energy and purpose. **"Today, we'll explore the art and science of problem-solving, focusing on best practices and techniques to optimize our problem-solving process. By understanding how IQ influences our approach to problem-solving and exploring proven strategies, we can**

overcome obstacles, seize opportunities, and achieve our goals."

She clicked the remote, and the screen displayed a quote: *"The best way to predict the future is to create it."* **"Let's begin by examining the essence of problem-solving techniques and their connection to IQ,"** Marvis continued. **"Problem-solving techniques encompass a range of approaches and methodologies for identifying, analyzing, and solving problems effectively."**

The next slide showcased examples of individuals who excel in problem-solving due to their high IQ and mastery of problem-solving techniques. **"Individuals with high IQs often demonstrate exceptional problem-solving skills,"** Marvis explained. **"They are adept at applying a variety of problem-solving techniques to tackle challenges with clarity, ingenuity, and resilience."**

A hand went up in the front row. **"How does IQ influence the effectiveness of problem-solving techniques?"**

Marvis nodded, acknowledging the question. **"Great question. IQ influences problem-solving by providing individuals with the cognitive resources and mental flexibility needed to apply problem-solving techniques effectively,"** she replied. **"Individuals with higher IQs tend to have stronger analytical skills, creative thinking abilities, and cognitive agility, enabling them to adapt problem-solving techniques to different contexts and challenges."**

She clicked to the next slide, which highlighted examples of problem-solving techniques where high IQ plays a crucial role. **"In real-world scenarios, individuals with high IQs often excel in tasks that require applying problem-solving techniques such as root cause analysis, brainstorming,** and decision trees," Marvis noted. "**They are skilled at selecting the most appropriate technique for the situation, leveraging their cognitive abilities to generate innovative solutions and make informed decisions.**"

The screen transitioned to examples of successful problem-solving endeavors led by individuals with high IQs and adept problem-solving techniques. "**From overcoming technical challenges to resolving interpersonal conflicts, individuals with high IQs have leveraged problem-solving techniques to navigate obstacles and achieve success,**" Marvis explained. "**Their ability to apply best practices and adapt their problem-solving approach to different situations has enabled them to overcome adversity and achieve their goals.**"

A hand went up in the middle row. "**What are some best practices for effective problem-solving?**"

Marvis considered the question thoughtfully. "**One best practice is to approach problems with a systematic and structured methodology, such as the problem-solving cycle or the scientific method,**" she replied. "**Additionally, fostering a collaborative and open-minded mindset, seeking diverse perspectives, and embracing failure as a learning opportunity can enhance problem-solving effectiveness and lead to more innovative solutions.**"

The final slide summarized the key takeaways from the discussion, emphasizing the importance of problem-solving techniques in leveraging IQ for success. "**In summary, problem-solving techniques are essential tools for harnessing the power of Intellectual Intelligence,**" Marvis concluded. "**By mastering best practices and applying proven strategies, individuals can overcome challenges, seize opportunities,**

and achieve their goals with confidence and precision."

She finished with a thought-provoking statement, her voice resonating with conviction. **"As we continue to explore the interplay between IQ and problem-solving techniques, let's challenge ourselves to adopt a proactive approach to problem-solving and unleash our full potential for innovation and achievement."**

The room filled with applause, the students clearly inspired and eager to apply the principles of problem-solving techniques and IQ in their own endeavors. Dr. Marvis Carter smiled, knowing she had equipped them with invaluable tools for navigating the complexities of the modern world with clarity and ingenuity.

7

Chapter 7: Emotional Intelligence in Personal Relationships

The Impact of EQ on Interpersonal Relationships

The atmosphere in the lecture hall shifted as Dr. Marvis Carter transitioned into the exploration of Emotional Intelligence (EQ) within the realm of personal relationships. She knew that delving into the impact of EQ on interpersonal dynamics would offer her students valuable insights into fostering meaningful connections, resolving conflicts, and nurturing fulfilling relationships.

"Welcome, everyone," Marvis began, her voice gentle yet resolute. **"Today, we embark on a journey to explore the profound influence of Emotional Intelligence on our personal relationships. By understanding how EQ shapes our interactions, communication, and connections with others, we can cultivate deeper empathy, trust, and harmony in our relationships."**

She clicked the remote, and the screen displayed a quote:

"The quality of our relationships determines the quality of our lives."
"Let's begin by examining the essence of Emotional Intelligence and its connection to interpersonal relationships," Marvis continued. "**Emotional Intelligence encompasses the ability to recognize, understand, and manage our own emotions, as well as the emotions of others.**"

The next slide showcased examples of individuals who excel in interpersonal relationships due to their high EQ and empathetic nature. "**Individuals with high EQs often demonstrate exceptional interpersonal skills,**" Marvis explained. "**They possess the empathy, self-awareness, and social competence needed to navigate the complexities of human relationships with grace and compassion.**"

A hand went up in the front row. "**How does EQ influence the dynamics of interpersonal relationships?**"

Marvis nodded, appreciating the question. "**Excellent question. EQ influences interpersonal relationships by providing individuals with the emotional intelligence needed to forge deeper connections, resolve conflicts constructively, and communicate effectively,**" she replied. "**Individuals with higher EQs tend to have greater empathy, emotional resilience, and interpersonal sensitivity, enabling them to build trust, foster collaboration, and nurture meaningful relationships.**"

She clicked to the next slide, which highlighted examples of interpersonal dynamics where high EQ plays a crucial role. "**In real-world relationships, individuals with high EQs often excel in tasks that require active listening, perspective-taking, and empathetic understanding,**" Marvis noted. "**They are skilled at navigating conflicts, expressing emotions authentically, and fostering a supportive** and nurturing environment for themselves and others."

The screen transitioned to examples of successful relationships led by individuals with high EQs and adept interpersonal skills. **"From romantic partnerships to friendships and familial bonds, individuals with high EQs have leveraged Emotional Intelligence to cultivate deep, meaningful connections with others,"** Marvis explained. **"Their ability to understand, empathize, and communicate effectively has fostered trust, intimacy, and mutual respect in their relationships."**

A hand went up in the middle row. **"How can individuals develop their Emotional Intelligence and enhance their interpersonal relationships?"**

Marvis considered the question thoughtfully. **"One approach is to practice self-awareness and emotional regulation techniques, such as mindfulness meditation and journaling, to deepen our understanding of our own emotions and reactions,"** she replied. **"Additionally, seeking feedback, practicing active listening, and cultivating empathy through volunteer work or community engagement can help individuals develop their Emotional Intelligence and foster healthier, more fulfilling relationships."**

The final slide summarized the key takeaways from the discussion, emphasizing the transformative impact of EQ on interpersonal dynamics. **"In summary, Emotional Intelligence is the cornerstone of healthy, fulfilling relationships,"** Marvis concluded. **"By nurturing our EQ and honing our interpersonal skills, we can create deeper connections, resolve conflicts peacefully, and cultivate relationships that enrich our lives and those of others."**

She finished with a thought-provoking statement, her voice

resonating with empathy. **"As we continue to explore the interplay between EQ and interpersonal relationships, let's challenge ourselves to cultivate compassion, empathy, and authenticity in our interactions, fostering a world where understanding and connection thrive."**

The room filled with quiet contemplation, the students clearly inspired and eager to apply the principles of Emotional Intelligence in their personal relationships. Dr. Marvis Carter smiled, knowing she had opened a doorway to deeper connections and more meaningful interactions in their lives.

Communication Skills and Emotional Intelligence

The lecture hall buzzed with anticipation as Dr. Marvis Carter delved deeper into the intricate connection between Emotional Intelligence (EQ) and communication skills within personal relationships. She knew that exploring how EQ influences communication would equip her students with the tools to express themselves authentically, navigate conflicts constructively, and foster deeper connections with others.

"Welcome back, everyone," Marvis began, her voice warm and inviting. **"Today, we continue our exploration of Emotional Intelligence in personal relationships by examining the pivotal role of communication skills. By understanding how EQ shapes our ability to express ourselves, listen actively, and connect with others, we can cultivate healthier, more fulfilling relationships."**

She clicked the remote, and the screen displayed a quote: *"Communication is the key to understanding."* **"Let's begin by exploring the essence of communication skills and their intimate relationship with Emotional Intelligence,"**

CHAPTER 7: EMOTIONAL INTELLIGENCE IN PERSONAL RELATIONSHIPS

Marvis continued. "**Communication skills encompass the ability to convey thoughts, feelings, and ideas effectively, as well as the capacity to listen empathetically and respond with sensitivity.**"

The next slide showcased examples of individuals who excel in communication due to their high EQ and empathetic nature. "**Individuals with high EQs often demonstrate exceptional communication skills,**" Marvis explained. "**They possess the empathy, emotional awareness, and social acumen needed to engage in meaningful dialogue, resolve conflicts, and build trust in their relationships.**"

A hand went up in the front row. "**How does EQ influence communication dynamics in personal relationships?**"

Marvis nodded, appreciating the question. "**Great question. EQ influences communication dynamics by providing individuals with the emotional intelligence needed to express themselves authentically, listen attentively, and navigate interpersonal interactions with empathy,**" she replied. "**Individuals with higher EQs tend to communicate more effectively, convey their emotions and needs clearly, and respond to others with understanding and respect, fostering deeper connections and mutual trust.**"

She clicked to the next slide, which highlighted examples of communication scenarios where high EQ plays a crucial role. "**In real-world relationships, individuals with high EQs often excel in tasks that require active listening, empathetic responding, and assertive communication,**" Marvis noted. "**They are skilled at expressing their thoughts and feelings assertively, validating others' emotions, and fostering open, honest communication that strengthens their relationships.**"

The screen transitioned to examples of successful communication in relationships led by individuals with high EQs and adept communication skills. "**From intimate conversations to difficult discussions and heartfelt apologies, individuals with high EQs leverage effective communication to deepen their connections and resolve conflicts constructively,**" Marvis explained. "**Their ability to express themselves authentically, listen with empathy, and communicate with clarity fosters mutual understanding and strengthens the bonds of trust and intimacy in their relationships.**"

A hand went up in the middle row. "**How can individuals develop their communication skills and enhance their Emotional Intelligence?**"

Marvis considered the question thoughtfully. "**One approach is to practice active listening, empathy, and assertiveness in our daily interactions with others,**" she replied. "**Additionally, seeking feedback, engaging in role-playing exercises, and attending communication workshops can help individuals refine their communication skills and deepen their Emotional Intelligence, leading to more meaningful and satisfying relationships.**"

The final slide summarized the key takeaways from the discussion, emphasizing the transformative impact of communication skills on interpersonal dynamics. "**In summary, effective communication is the cornerstone of healthy, fulfilling relationships,**" Marvis concluded. "**By nurturing our Emotional Intelligence and honing our communication skills, we can foster deeper connections, resolve conflicts peacefully, and create relationships that enrich our lives and those of others.**"

She finished with a thought-provoking statement, her voice resonating with warmth and encouragement. **"As we continue to explore the interplay between EQ and communication skills, let's challenge ourselves to communicate with authenticity, empathy, and compassion, creating spaces where understanding and connection flourish."**

The room filled with quiet reflection, the students clearly inspired and eager to apply the principles of Emotional Intelligence in their communication and relationships. Dr. Marvis Carter smiled, knowing she had empowered them to foster deeper connections and build more meaningful bonds in their lives.

Managing Emotions in Relationships

The lecture hall hummed with anticipation as Dr. Marvis Carter delved deeper into the intricacies of Emotional Intelligence (EQ) and its role in managing emotions within personal relationships. She knew that exploring how EQ influences emotional regulation would provide her students with invaluable insights into fostering harmony, understanding, and resilience in their interactions with others.

"Welcome back, everyone," Marvis began, her voice gentle yet authoritative. **"Today, we continue our exploration of Emotional Intelligence by examining the vital importance of managing emotions within personal relationships. By understanding how EQ shapes our ability to regulate emotions, empathize with others, and maintain healthy boundaries, we can cultivate deeper connections and navigate challenges with grace and compassion."**

She clicked the remote, and the screen displayed a quote:

"Emotions are the language of the soul." **"Let's begin by exploring the essence of managing emotions and its profound connection to Emotional Intelligence,"** Marvis continued. **"Managing emotions involves the ability to recognize, understand, and regulate our own emotions, as well as the emotions of others, in order to foster positive interactions and maintain healthy relationships."**

The next slide showcased examples of individuals who excel in managing emotions due to their high EQ and self-awareness. **"Individuals with high EQs often demonstrate exceptional emotional regulation skills,"** Marvis explained. **"They possess the self-awareness, empathy, and resilience needed to navigate the ebb and flow of emotions in their relationships with poise and empathy."**

A hand went up in the front row. **"How does EQ influence the management of emotions in personal relationships?"**

Marvis nodded, appreciating the question. **"An excellent question. EQ influences the management of emotions by providing individuals with the emotional intelligence needed to recognize and regulate their own emotions, as well as empathize with and support others in managing their emotions,"** she replied. **"Individuals with higher EQs tend to have greater emotional self-awareness, self-regulation, and empathy, enabling them to navigate conflicts, communicate effectively, and maintain healthy boundaries in their relationships."**

She clicked to the next slide, which highlighted examples of emotional management scenarios where high EQ plays a crucial role. **"In real-world relationships, individuals with high EQs often excel in tasks that require navigating challenging emotions, resolving conflicts peacefully, and** providing support and empathy to their loved ones," Marvis noted. "**They are skilled at recognizing triggers, managing stress, and responding to emotions with empathy and understanding, fostering resilience and harmony in their relationships.**"

The screen transitioned to examples of successful emotional management in relationships led by individuals with high EQs and adept emotional regulation skills. "**From moments of vulnerability to times of conflict and uncertainty, individuals with high EQs leverage emotional management to foster trust, empathy, and resilience in their relationships,**" Marvis explained. "**Their ability to regulate their own emotions, empathize with others, and maintain healthy boundaries creates a safe and supportive environment where emotions can be expressed and understood with compassion and respect.**"

A hand went up in the middle row. "**How can individuals develop their emotional regulation skills and enhance their Emotional Intelligence?**"

Marvis considered the question thoughtfully. "**One approach is to practice mindfulness, self-reflection, and relaxation techniques to cultivate emotional self-awareness and regulation,**" she replied. "**Additionally, seeking support from trusted friends or therapists, developing healthy coping mechanisms, and setting clear boundaries in our relationships can help individuals manage their emotions more effectively and deepen their Emotional Intelligence.**"

The final slide summarized the key takeaways from the discussion, emphasizing the transformative impact of emotional management on personal relationships. "**In summary,**

managing emotions is essential for fostering healthy, resilient relationships," Marvis concluded. **"By nurturing our Emotional Intelligence and honing our emotional regulation skills, we can cultivate deeper connections, navigate conflicts with grace, and create relationships that nurture our emotional well-being and growth."**

She finished with a thought-provoking statement, her voice resonating with empathy and encouragement. **"As we continue to explore the interplay between EQ and emotional management, let's challenge ourselves to cultivate compassion, resilience, and empathy in our relationships, creating spaces where emotions are honored, understood, and embraced."**

The room filled with a sense of understanding and determination, the students clearly inspired and eager to apply the principles of Emotional Intelligence in managing their emotions and fostering healthier relationships. Dr. Marvis Carter smiled, knowing she had equipped them with invaluable tools for navigating the complexities of human connection with wisdom and compassion.

Building Empathy and Understanding

The lecture hall brimmed with anticipation as Dr. Marvis Carter delved into the profound connection between Emotional Intelligence (EQ) and the cultivation of empathy and understanding within personal relationships. She knew that exploring how EQ influences empathy would offer her students invaluable insights into fostering deeper connections, resolving conflicts, and nurturing compassion in their interactions with others.

CHAPTER 7: EMOTIONAL INTELLIGENCE IN PERSONAL RELATIONSHIPS

"**Welcome back, everyone,**" Marvis began, her voice resonating with warmth and compassion. "**Today, we continue our exploration of Emotional Intelligence by delving into the transformative power of empathy and understanding in personal relationships. By understanding how EQ shapes our capacity for empathy, we can cultivate deeper connections, foster mutual understanding, and nurture compassion in our interactions with others.**"

She clicked the remote, and the screen displayed a quote: *"Empathy is the bridge that connects hearts."* "**Let's begin by exploring the essence of empathy and its profound connection to Emotional Intelligence,**" Marvis continued. "**Empathy encompasses the ability to understand and share the feelings of others, to see the world through their eyes, and to respond with compassion and kindness.**"

The next slide showcased examples of individuals who excel in empathy due to their high EQ and empathetic nature. "**Individuals with high EQs often demonstrate exceptional empathy and understanding,**" Marvis explained. "**They possess the emotional intelligence needed to recognize and validate the emotions of others, to listen with compassion, and to offer support and understanding in times of need.**"

A hand went up in the front row. "**How does EQ influence the development of empathy in personal relationships?**"

Marvis nodded, appreciating the question. "**An excellent question. EQ influences the development of empathy by providing individuals with the emotional intelligence needed to recognize and understand the emotions of others, as well as to respond with compassion and empathy,**" she replied. "**Individuals with higher EQs tend to have greater emotional awareness, perspective-taking abilities,** and interpersonal sensitivity, enabling them to cultivate deeper connections and foster mutual understanding in their relationships."

She clicked to the next slide, which highlighted examples of empathy-building scenarios where high EQ plays a crucial role. "**In real-world relationships, individuals with high EQs often excel in tasks that require empathetic listening, validation of emotions, and offering support and understanding,**" Marvis noted. "**They are skilled at tuning into the emotions of others, recognizing their needs, and responding with empathy and compassion, creating a safe and supportive space for emotional expression and connection.**"

The screen transitioned to examples of successful relationships led by individuals with high EQs and cultivated empathy. "**From moments of joy to times of sorrow and uncertainty, individuals with high EQs leverage empathy and understanding to foster deeper connections and nurture mutual support in their relationships,**" Marvis explained. "**Their ability to empathize with others, validate their experiences, and offer support without judgment creates a foundation of trust and mutual respect that strengthens their relationships.**"

A hand went up in the middle row. "**How can individuals develop their empathy and understanding skills and enhance their Emotional Intelligence?**"

Marvis considered the question thoughtfully. "**One approach is to practice active listening, perspective-taking, and empathetic responding in our interactions with others,**" she replied. "**Additionally, seeking to understand different perspectives, engaging in empathy-building** exercises, and cultivating a mindset of compassion and kindness can help individuals develop their empathy and understanding skills and deepen their Emotional Intelligence."

The final slide summarized the key takeaways from the discussion, emphasizing the transformative impact of empathy and understanding on personal relationships. "**In summary, empathy is the cornerstone of healthy, fulfilling relationships,**" Marvis concluded. "**By nurturing our Emotional Intelligence and cultivating empathy and understanding, we can create deeper connections, foster mutual support, and cultivate a culture of compassion and kindness in our relationships.**"

She finished with a thought-provoking statement, her voice resonating with empathy and encouragement. "**As we continue to explore the interplay between EQ and empathy, let's challenge ourselves to cultivate empathy and understanding in our interactions, creating spaces where hearts are connected, and souls are uplifted.**"

The room filled with a sense of empathy and determination, the students clearly inspired and eager to apply the principles of Emotional Intelligence in fostering deeper connections and nurturing compassion in their relationships. Dr. Marvis Carter smiled, knowing she had ignited a spark of empathy and understanding that would ripple through their lives and the lives of those around them.

Conflict Management and Resolution

The lecture hall buzzed with anticipation as Dr. Marvis Carter delved deeper into the intricate connection between Emotional Intelligence (EQ) and conflict management within personal relationships. She knew that exploring how EQ influences conflict resolution would offer her students invaluable insights into navigating disagreements, fostering compromise, and strengthening relationships.

"**Welcome back, everyone,**" Marvis began, her voice steady yet empathetic. "**Today, we continue our exploration of Emotional Intelligence by examining the pivotal role of conflict management and resolution in personal relationships. By understanding how EQ shapes our approach to conflict, we can navigate disagreements with empathy, assertiveness, and grace, fostering understanding and strengthening our connections with others.**"

She clicked the remote, and the screen displayed a quote: *"In the midst of conflict, lies opportunity."* "**Let's begin by exploring the essence of conflict management and its profound connection to Emotional Intelligence,**" Marvis continued. "**Conflict management involves the ability to identify, address, and resolve conflicts constructively, while preserving the dignity and respect of all parties involved.**"

The next slide showcased examples of individuals who excel in conflict resolution due to their high EQ and diplomatic nature. "**Individuals with high EQs often demonstrate exceptional conflict resolution skills,**" Marvis explained. "**They possess the emotional intelligence needed to remain calm under pressure, listen actively to all perspectives, and**

CHAPTER 7: EMOTIONAL INTELLIGENCE IN PERSONAL RELATIONSHIPS

find mutually beneficial solutions to conflicts, fostering harmony and understanding in their relationships."

A hand went up in the front row. "How does EQ influence the management of conflicts in personal relationships?"

Marvis nodded, appreciating the question. "**An excellent question. EQ influences conflict management by providing individuals with the emotional intelligence needed to understand their own emotions and reactions, as well as those of others, in the heat of conflict,**" she replied. "**Individuals with higher EQs tend to have greater emotional self-regulation, empathy, and interpersonal skills, enabling them to navigate conflicts with empathy, assertiveness, and resilience, fostering resolution and growth in their relationships.**"

She clicked to the next slide, which highlighted examples of conflict resolution scenarios where high EQ plays a crucial role. "**In real-world relationships, individuals with high EQs often excel in tasks that require active listening, empathy, and compromise,**" Marvis noted. "**They are skilled at de-escalating tensions, reframing perspectives, and finding common ground, leading to resolution and reconciliation in even the most challenging conflicts.**"

The screen transitioned to examples of successful conflict resolution in relationships led by individuals with high EQs and adept conflict management skills. "**From disagreements over finances to conflicts over values and priorities, individuals with high EQs leverage conflict resolution techniques to foster understanding, compromise, and growth in their relationships,**" Marvis explained. "**Their ability to remain calm under pressure, communicate assertively, and seek win-win solutions creates a foundation** of trust and respect that strengthens their connections with others."

A hand went up in the middle row. "**How can individuals develop their conflict management skills and enhance their Emotional Intelligence?**"

Marvis considered the question thoughtfully. "**One approach is to practice active listening, empathy, and assertiveness in our communication during conflicts,**" she replied. "**Additionally, seeking to understand the underlying needs and interests of all parties involved, reframing conflicts as opportunities for growth and learning, and seeking guidance from mediation or conflict resolution experts can help individuals develop their conflict management skills and deepen their Emotional Intelligence.**"

The final slide summarized the key takeaways from the discussion, emphasizing the transformative impact of conflict management on personal relationships. "**In summary, conflict management is essential for fostering healthy, resilient relationships,**" Marvis concluded. "**By nurturing our Emotional Intelligence and honing our conflict resolution skills, we can navigate disagreements with empathy and grace, fostering understanding and strengthening our connections with others.**"

She finished with a thought-provoking statement, her voice resonating with empathy and determination. "**As we continue to explore the interplay between EQ and conflict management, let's challenge ourselves to approach conflicts with empathy, assertiveness, and a willingness to seek understanding, creating spaces where conflicts become opportunities for growth and connection.**"

The room filled with a sense of empowerment and resolve,

the students clearly inspired and eager to apply the principles of Emotional Intelligence in navigating conflicts and fostering stronger relationships. Dr. Marvis Carter smiled, knowing she had equipped them with invaluable tools for fostering understanding and harmony in their interactions with others.

Strengthening Bonds with Emotional Awareness

The lecture hall was alive with anticipation as Dr. Marvis Carter delved into the profound connection between Emotional Intelligence (EQ) and the strengthening of bonds through emotional awareness within personal relationships. She knew that exploring how EQ influences emotional awareness would offer her students invaluable insights into deepening connections, fostering intimacy, and nurturing lasting bonds with others.

"**Welcome back, everyone,**" Marvis began, her voice filled with warmth and sincerity. "**Today, we conclude our exploration of Emotional Intelligence by delving into the transformative power of emotional awareness in personal relationships. By understanding how EQ shapes our ability to recognize, express, and respond to emotions, we can cultivate deeper connections, foster intimacy, and nurture bonds that withstand the test of time.**"

She clicked the remote, and the screen displayed a quote: *"Emotional awareness is the foundation of authentic connection."* "**Let's begin by exploring the essence of emotional awareness and its profound connection to Emotional Intelligence,**" Marvis continued. "**Emotional awareness involves the ability to recognize and understand our own emotions, as well as the emotions of others, and to respond** with empathy, authenticity, and vulnerability."

The next slide showcased examples of individuals who excel in emotional awareness due to their high EQ and introspective nature. "**Individuals with high EQs often demonstrate exceptional emotional awareness,**" Marvis explained. "**They possess the emotional intelligence needed to tune into their own emotions, as well as the emotions of others, with sensitivity and compassion, fostering deeper connections and intimacy in their relationships.**"

A hand went up in the front row. "**How does EQ influence the development of emotional awareness in personal relationships?**"

Marvis nodded, appreciating the question. "**An excellent question. EQ influences the development of emotional awareness by providing individuals with the emotional intelligence needed to recognize and understand their own emotions, as well as the emotions of others, in the context of their relationships,**" she replied. "**Individuals with higher EQs tend to have greater self-awareness, empathy, and emotional regulation skills, enabling them to cultivate deeper connections and foster intimacy through authentic emotional expression and vulnerability.**"

She clicked to the next slide, which highlighted examples of emotional awareness scenarios where high EQ plays a crucial role. "**In real-world relationships, individuals with high EQs often excel in tasks that require emotional attunement, empathetic responding, and vulnerability,**" Marvis noted. "**They are skilled at expressing their emotions authentically, validating the emotions of others, and creating a safe and supportive space for emotional expression and connection.**"

CHAPTER 7: EMOTIONAL INTELLIGENCE IN PERSONAL RELATIONSHIPS

The screen transitioned to examples of successful relationships led by individuals with high EQs and cultivated emotional awareness. **"From moments of joy and celebration to times of sadness and uncertainty, individuals with high EQs leverage emotional awareness to foster intimacy, vulnerability, and trust in their relationships,"** Marvis explained. **"Their ability to tune into their own emotions and the emotions of others, and to respond with empathy and authenticity, creates a bond of understanding and connection that strengthens their relationships."**

A hand went up in the middle row. **"How can individuals develop their emotional awareness and enhance their Emotional Intelligence?"**

Marvis considered the question thoughtfully. **"One approach is to practice self-reflection, mindfulness, and journaling to cultivate self-awareness and emotional literacy,"** she replied. **"Additionally, seeking feedback from trusted friends or therapists, engaging in deep conversations that explore emotions and vulnerabilities, and embracing authenticity and vulnerability in our relationships can help individuals develop their emotional awareness and deepen their Emotional Intelligence."**

The final slide summarized the key takeaways from the discussion, emphasizing the transformative impact of emotional awareness on personal relationships. **"In summary, emotional awareness is the cornerstone of authentic, intimate connections,"** Marvis concluded. **"By nurturing our Emotional Intelligence and honing our emotional awareness, we can cultivate deeper bonds, foster intimacy, and create relationships that enrich our lives and those of others."**

She finished with a thought-provoking statement, her voice resonating with empathy and encouragement. **"As we conclude our exploration of EQ and personal relationships, let's challenge ourselves to cultivate emotional awareness and vulnerability in our interactions, creating spaces where authenticity thrives, and connections deepen."**

The room filled with a sense of understanding and acceptance, the students clearly inspired and eager to apply the principles of Emotional Intelligence in deepening their connections and fostering more meaningful relationships. Dr. Marvis Carter smiled, knowing she had empowered them to embrace their emotions and forge bonds that would last a lifetime.

8

Chapter 8: The Workplace: IQ and EQ at Work

The Role of IQ in Job Performance

The conference room was abuzz with anticipation as Dr. Marvis Carter stepped to the front, ready to delve into the intricate dynamics of IQ and EQ in the workplace. She knew that exploring the role of IQ in job performance would provide invaluable insights into understanding how cognitive abilities shape professional success.

"**Welcome, everyone,**" Marvis began, her voice commanding attention. "**Today, we embark on a journey to explore the interplay between IQ and EQ in the workplace. We start by examining the pivotal role of IQ—Intellectual Quotient—in determining job performance and success.**"

She clicked the remote, and the screen illuminated with a quote: *"Intelligence without ambition is a bird without wings."* "**Let's begin by exploring the essence of IQ and its impact on job performance,**" Marvis continued. "**IQ refers to our** cognitive abilities, including reasoning, problem-solving, and analytical skills, which are crucial for mastering tasks, adapting to challenges, and achieving success in the workplace."

The next slide showcased examples of individuals who excel in their careers due to their high IQ and analytical prowess. "**Individuals with high IQs often demonstrate exceptional performance in their jobs,**" Marvis explained. "**They possess the cognitive abilities needed to grasp complex concepts, solve intricate problems, and innovate in their respective fields, driving productivity and success in the workplace.**"

A hand went up in the front row. "**How does IQ influence job performance across different industries?**"

Marvis nodded, appreciating the question. "**An excellent question. IQ influences job performance by providing individuals with the cognitive abilities needed to excel in their specific roles and industries,**" she replied. "**In fields such as engineering, finance, and technology, where analytical thinking and problem-solving are paramount, individuals with higher IQs tend to perform exceptionally well, driving innovation and efficiency in their organizations.**"

She clicked to the next slide, which highlighted examples of job performance scenarios where high IQ plays a crucial role. "**In real-world workplaces, individuals with high IQs often excel in tasks that require critical thinking, data analysis, and strategic decision-making,**" Marvis noted. "**They are skilled at synthesizing information, identifying patterns, and devising effective solutions to complex challenges, contributing to the success and growth of** their organizations."

The screen transitioned to examples of successful professionals whose high IQs have propelled them to leadership positions and achievements in their respective fields. "**From engineering marvels to groundbreaking research and financial innovations, individuals with high IQs leverage their cognitive abilities to drive progress and success in their careers,**" Marvis explained. "**Their ability to think critically, solve problems creatively, and adapt to new challenges positions them as leaders and innovators in their industries.**"

A hand went up in the middle row. "**How can individuals leverage their IQ to enhance their job performance and professional success?**"

Marvis considered the question thoughtfully. "**One approach is to continuously challenge oneself with intellectually stimulating tasks and projects, seeking opportunities for learning and growth,**" she replied. "**Additionally, developing strong analytical and problem-solving skills, staying informed about industry trends and advancements, and seeking mentorship or training can help individuals leverage their IQ and achieve greater success in their careers.**"

The final slide summarized the key takeaways from the discussion, emphasizing the pivotal role of IQ in job performance and success. "**In summary, IQ is a key determinant of job performance, driving productivity, innovation, and success in the workplace,**" Marvis concluded. "**By nurturing our cognitive abilities and honing our analytical skills, we can excel in our roles, contribute to the growth of our organizations, and achieve our professional aspirations.**"

She finished with a thought-provoking statement, her voice resonating with determination and ambition. **"As we continue to explore the interplay between IQ and EQ in the workplace, let's challenge ourselves to harness our cognitive abilities and strive for excellence, creating opportunities for growth and advancement in our careers."**

The room filled with a sense of purpose and ambition, the audience clearly inspired and eager to apply the principles of IQ to enhance their job performance and professional success. Dr. Marvis Carter smiled, knowing she had ignited a spark of motivation and determination that would propel them to new heights in their careers.

EQ and Team Dynamics

The atmosphere in the conference room shifted as Dr. Marvis Carter transitioned seamlessly from discussing IQ to exploring the intricate dynamics of Emotional Intelligence (EQ) and its impact on team dynamics in the workplace. She knew that understanding how EQ influences collaboration and communication would provide invaluable insights into fostering effective teamwork and organizational success.

"Now, let's turn our attention to Emotional Intelligence," Marvis began, her voice conveying a sense of anticipation. **"We'll explore how EQ shapes team dynamics and contributes to organizational success."**

She clicked the remote, and the screen displayed a quote: *"Alone we can do so little; together we can do so much."* **"Let's begin by exploring the essence of EQ and its impact on team dynamics,"** Marvis continued. **"EQ refers to our ability to recognize, understand, and manage our own emotions, as** well as the emotions of others, in order to navigate social interactions effectively."

The next slide showcased examples of individuals who excel in teamwork due to their high EQ and interpersonal skills. **"Individuals with high EQs often demonstrate exceptional abilities in fostering collaboration and teamwork,"** Marvis explained. **"They possess the emotional intelligence needed to communicate effectively, build trust, and resolve conflicts, creating a cohesive and productive team environment."**

A hand went up in the front row. **"How does EQ influence team dynamics and performance?"**

Marvis nodded, appreciating the question. **"An excellent question. EQ influences team dynamics by providing individuals with the emotional intelligence needed to understand and navigate the emotions of their team members,"** she replied. **"In team settings, individuals with higher EQs tend to foster open communication, empathy, and mutual respect, leading to increased trust, cooperation, and innovation within the team."**

She clicked to the next slide, which highlighted examples of team dynamics scenarios where high EQ plays a crucial role. **"In real-world workplaces, teams led by individuals with high EQs often excel in tasks that require collaboration, creativity, and adaptability,"** Marvis noted. **"They are skilled at building rapport, resolving conflicts constructively, and leveraging the diverse strengths of team members, leading to higher performance and achievement of organizational goals."**

The screen transitioned to examples of successful teams whose high EQ has propelled them to success in achieving their objectives and fostering a positive work culture. **"From cross-functional projects to high-stakes initiatives, teams with high EQs leverage their emotional intelligence to navigate challenges, capitalize on opportunities, and achieve outstanding results,"** Marvis explained. **"Their ability to communicate effectively, collaborate seamlessly, and support one another fosters a culture of trust, innovation, and excellence within the organization."**

A hand went up in the middle row. **"How can organizations foster EQ in their teams and enhance team dynamics?"**

Marvis considered the question thoughtfully. **"One approach is to provide training and development opportunities focused on emotional intelligence, communication, and conflict resolution skills,"** she replied. **"Additionally, creating a supportive and inclusive work environment, promoting psychological safety, and recognizing and valuing the contributions of team members can help foster EQ in teams and enhance their dynamics, leading to greater cohesion and performance."**

The final slide summarized the key takeaways from the discussion, emphasizing the transformative impact of EQ on team dynamics and organizational success. **"In summary, EQ is a key driver of effective teamwork and organizational performance,"** Marvis concluded. **"By nurturing our emotional intelligence and fostering a culture of collaboration and empathy, organizations can unlock the full potential of their teams and achieve extraordinary results."**

She finished with a thought-provoking statement, her voice resonating with optimism and determination. **"As we continue to explore the interplay between IQ and EQ in the workplace, let's challenge ourselves to cultivate emotional** intelligence and foster effective teamwork, creating environments where every individual thrives, and teams achieve greatness."

The room filled with a sense of camaraderie and unity, the audience clearly inspired and eager to apply the principles of EQ to enhance their team dynamics and organizational success. Dr. Marvis Carter smiled, knowing she had empowered them to foster a culture of collaboration and empathy that would drive their organizations to new heights.

Hiring for EQ vs. IQ: What to Look For

As the discussion on Emotional Intelligence (EQ) and its impact on team dynamics unfolded, Dr. Marvis Carter seamlessly transitioned to the critical topic of hiring and the balance between EQ and IQ in the recruitment process. She knew that understanding what to look for in candidates would provide invaluable insights into building high-performing teams and fostering a positive work culture.

"**Now, let's delve into the realm of hiring and explore the balance between EQ and IQ,**" Marvis began, her voice filled with gravitas. "**We'll examine what to consider when evaluating candidates for their Emotional Intelligence and Intellectual Quotient.**"

She clicked the remote, and the screen illuminated with a quote: *"Choose character over talent; choose EQ over IQ."* "**Let's begin by understanding the importance of both EQ and IQ in the hiring process,**" Marvis continued. "**EQ and IQ each play crucial roles in determining an individual's suitability for a role, and finding the right balance between the two is essential for building successful teams.**"

The next slide showcased examples of candidates who excel in their roles due to a balance of EQ and IQ. **"Candidates with a balance of EQ and IQ often demonstrate exceptional performance and fit within their respective roles and organizations,"** Marvis explained. **"They possess the cognitive abilities needed to excel in their tasks, as well as the emotional intelligence required to collaborate effectively, communicate persuasively, and adapt to the dynamic demands of the workplace."**

A hand went up in the front row. **"How do you determine the right balance of EQ and IQ in candidates?"**

Marvis nodded, appreciating the question. **"An excellent question. Evaluating the balance of EQ and IQ in candidates requires a holistic approach,"** she replied. **"It involves assessing their cognitive abilities, problem-solving skills, and technical competencies, as well as their interpersonal skills, communication style, and emotional intelligence."**

She clicked to the next slide, which highlighted examples of qualities to look for in candidates when assessing EQ and IQ. **"When evaluating EQ, look for qualities such as empathy, self-awareness, resilience, and interpersonal skills,"** Marvis noted. **"Candidates who demonstrate emotional intelligence are often able to navigate challenges, build relationships, and contribute positively to team dynamics."**

The screen transitioned to examples of successful hires who possess both high EQ and IQ, contributing significantly to their organizations' success. **"From innovative problem solvers to effective communicators and collaborative team players, individuals with a balance of EQ and IQ bring a diverse set of skills and perspectives to their roles,"**

Marvis explained. "**Their ability to understand and manage their emotions, as well as effectively engage with others, makes them invaluable assets to their organizations.**"

A hand went up in the middle row. "**How can organizations ensure they are hiring for both EQ and IQ effectively?**"

Marvis considered the question thoughtfully. "**One approach is to incorporate behavioral assessments, structured interviews, and situational judgment tests into the hiring process to evaluate both cognitive abilities and emotional intelligence,**" she replied. "**Additionally, providing training and development opportunities to enhance both EQ and IQ in existing employees can help foster a culture of continuous growth and development within the organization.**"

The final slide summarized the key takeaways from the discussion, emphasizing the importance of balancing EQ and IQ in the hiring process for building high-performing teams and fostering a positive work culture. "**In summary, hiring for both EQ and IQ is essential for building successful teams and driving organizational success,**" Marvis concluded. "**By evaluating candidates holistically and prioritizing qualities such as emotional intelligence, organizations can ensure they are selecting individuals who not only excel in their roles but also contribute positively to the overall culture and success of the organization.**"

She finished with a thought-provoking statement, her voice resonating with insight and determination. "**As we continue to explore the interplay between EQ and IQ in the workplace, let's challenge ourselves to prioritize both cognitive abilities and emotional intelligence in our hiring decisions, creating environments where every** individual thrives, and teams achieve greatness."

The room filled with a sense of purpose and clarity, the audience clearly inspired and eager to apply the principles of balanced hiring to build high-performing teams and foster a positive work culture. Dr. Marvis Carter smiled, knowing she had empowered them to make informed decisions that would drive their organizations' success.

Enhancing Workplace Culture with EQ

As the discussion unfolded on the interplay between Emotional Intelligence (EQ) and Intellectual Quotient (IQ) in the workplace, Dr. Marvis Carter shifted the focus to the critical role of EQ in shaping organizational culture. She knew that understanding how EQ enhances workplace culture would provide invaluable insights into fostering a positive and productive work environment.

"**Now, let's explore how Emotional Intelligence can enhance workplace culture,**" Marvis began, her voice carrying a tone of anticipation. "**We'll examine the transformative impact of EQ on fostering collaboration, communication, and cohesion within organizations.**"

She clicked the remote, and the screen illuminated with a quote: *"Culture eats strategy for breakfast."* "**Let's begin by understanding the essence of EQ and its influence on workplace culture,**" Marvis continued. "**EQ refers to our ability to recognize, understand, and manage our own emotions, as well as the emotions of others, in order to navigate social interactions effectively.**"

The next slide showcased examples of organizations that prioritize EQ and foster a positive work culture. "**Organizations** that prioritize Emotional Intelligence often cultivate a positive and inclusive work culture," Marvis explained. "They create environments where employees feel valued, supported, and empowered to bring their whole selves to work, leading to higher engagement, satisfaction, and productivity."

A hand went up in the front row. "**How does EQ contribute to shaping workplace culture?**"

Marvis nodded, appreciating the question. "**An excellent question. EQ contributes to shaping workplace culture by fostering empathy, collaboration, and trust among employees,**" she replied. "**In organizations where Emotional Intelligence is valued, employees feel heard, understood, and respected, leading to stronger relationships, effective communication, and a sense of belonging within the workplace.**"

She clicked to the next slide, which highlighted examples of qualities that contribute to a positive work culture fostered by EQ. "**When EQ is prioritized, organizations exhibit qualities such as empathy, authenticity, transparency, and inclusivity,**" Marvis noted. "**These qualities create a culture where diversity is celebrated, feedback is valued, and innovation thrives, leading to greater resilience and adaptability in the face of challenges.**"

The screen transitioned to examples of successful organizations known for their positive work culture driven by high levels of EQ among employees and leaders. "**From startup unicorns to Fortune 500 companies, organizations that prioritize Emotional Intelligence create environments where employees feel motivated, engaged, and empowered to contribute their best,**" Marvis explained. "**Their commitment to fostering a positive work culture sets them apart as employers of choice, attracting top talent and driving sustainable success."

A hand went up in the middle row. "**How can organizations enhance workplace culture with EQ?**"

Marvis considered the question thoughtfully. "**One approach is to lead by example, with leaders demonstrating and championing the values of Emotional Intelligence in their interactions and decision-making,**" she replied. "**Additionally, providing training and development opportunities focused on EQ, promoting open communication and psychological safety, and recognizing and rewarding behaviors that align with the organization's values can help cultivate a positive work culture driven by Emotional Intelligence.**"

The final slide summarized the key takeaways from the discussion, emphasizing the transformative impact of EQ on workplace culture and organizational success. "**In summary, EQ is a powerful force for enhancing workplace culture, fostering collaboration, communication, and cohesion within organizations,**" Marvis concluded. "**By prioritizing Emotional Intelligence and creating environments where employees feel valued and empowered, organizations can cultivate a positive and inclusive work culture that drives employee engagement, satisfaction, and performance.**"

She finished with a thought-provoking statement, her voice resonating with optimism and determination. "**As we continue to explore the interplay between IQ and EQ in the workplace, let's challenge ourselves to prioritize Emotional Intelligence and foster a culture where every individual thrives, and the organization achieves its full**

potential."

The room filled with a sense of inspiration and purpose, the audience clearly motivated and eager to apply the principles of EQ to enhance workplace culture and drive organizational success. Dr. Marvis Carter smiled, knowing she had empowered them to create environments where employees thrive and organizations flourish.

Balancing IQ and EQ in Professional Development

With the discussion on Emotional Intelligence (EQ) and its impact on workplace culture concluded, Dr. Marvis Carter turned her attention to the crucial topic of balancing IQ and EQ in professional development. She knew that understanding how to nurture both cognitive abilities and emotional intelligence would provide invaluable insights into fostering well-rounded and resilient professionals.

"Now, let's explore the importance of balancing IQ and EQ in professional development," Marvis began, her voice carrying a tone of conviction. **"We'll examine how organizations can support employees in developing both cognitive abilities and emotional intelligence to thrive in their careers."**

She clicked the remote, and the screen illuminated with a quote: *"The best investment you can make is in yourself."* **"Let's begin by understanding the significance of balancing IQ and EQ in professional growth,"** Marvis continued. **"IQ and EQ each contribute unique strengths to an individual's professional success, and finding the right balance between the two is essential for fostering resilience, adaptability, and growth."**

The next slide showcased examples of professionals who excel in their careers due to a balance of IQ and EQ. **"Professionals who balance IQ and EQ often demonstrate exceptional performance and leadership in their respective fields,"** Marvis explained. **"They possess the cognitive abilities needed to excel in their roles, as well as the emotional intelligence required to navigate challenges, build relationships, and lead effectively."**

A hand went up in the front row. **"How can individuals develop both IQ and EQ in their professional development?"**

Marvis nodded, appreciating the question. **"An excellent question. Developing both IQ and EQ requires a multifaceted approach,"** she replied. **"It involves seeking opportunities for continuous learning and skill development, as well as cultivating self-awareness, empathy, and interpersonal skills through self-reflection, feedback, and practice."**

She clicked to the next slide, which highlighted examples of strategies to balance IQ and EQ in professional development. **"When balancing IQ and EQ, individuals can focus on developing technical competencies, critical thinking skills, and problem-solving abilities, as well as emotional intelligence competencies such as self-awareness, social awareness, and relationship management,"** Marvis noted. **"By integrating both cognitive and emotional skills into their professional growth plans, individuals can become well-rounded and resilient professionals."**

The screen transitioned to examples of successful professionals who have mastered both IQ and EQ, achieving significant milestones in their careers and making a positive impact in their organizations. "**From innovative entrepreneurs to compassionate leaders and collaborative team players, individuals who balance IQ and EQ leverage their diverse skill sets to drive success and create positive change in their fields,**" Marvis explained. "**Their ability to navigate complex challenges, inspire others, and foster meaningful connections positions them as role models for professional development.**"

A hand went up in the middle row. "**How can organizations support employees in balancing IQ and EQ in their professional development?**"

Marvis considered the question thoughtfully. "**One approach is to provide a range of learning and development opportunities that address both cognitive and emotional intelligence competencies,**" she replied. "**Additionally, fostering a culture of continuous feedback and growth, promoting mentorship and coaching relationships, and recognizing and rewarding behaviors that demonstrate both IQ and EQ can help support employees in their professional development journey.**"

The final slide summarized the key takeaways from the discussion, emphasizing the importance of balancing IQ and EQ in professional growth for fostering resilience, adaptability, and success. "**In summary, balancing IQ and EQ in professional development is essential for nurturing well-rounded and resilient professionals,**" Marvis concluded. "**By integrating both cognitive and emotional skills into their growth plans, individuals can thrive in their careers, contribute meaningfully to their organizations, and achieve their full potential.**"

She finished with a thought-provoking statement, her voice

resonating with optimism and determination. **"As we continue to explore the interplay between IQ and EQ in the workplace, let's challenge ourselves to prioritize both cognitive abilities and emotional intelligence in our professional development efforts, creating pathways for growth, fulfillment, and success."**

The room filled with a sense of empowerment and inspiration, the audience clearly motivated and eager to apply the principles of balanced professional development to advance their careers and make a positive impact in their organizations. Dr. Marvis Carter smiled, knowing she had equipped them with the tools to thrive in an ever-evolving professional landscape.

Case Studies: Successful Organizations with High EQ

As Dr. Marvis Carter delved deeper into the discussion on Emotional Intelligence (EQ) and its impact on the workplace, she turned her attention to real-life examples of successful organizations that prioritize EQ. She knew that examining case studies would provide tangible insights into how EQ drives organizational success and fosters a positive work culture.

"Now, let's explore case studies of successful organizations that exemplify the power of Emotional Intelligence," Marvis began, her voice filled with enthusiasm. **"We'll examine how these companies leverage EQ to drive innovation, collaboration, and excellence within their teams and across their industries."**

She clicked the remote, and the screen illuminated with the logos of renowned organizations known for their high

EQ and positive work culture: **Google, Microsoft, and Zappos.** "Let's begin by examining Google," Marvis continued. **"Google is renowned for its commitment to fostering a culture of innovation, collaboration, and employee well-being. The company places a strong emphasis on Emotional Intelligence in its hiring process, seeking candidates who demonstrate empathy, adaptability, and resilience."**

The next slide showcased examples of initiatives at Google that promote EQ, such as mindfulness training, emotional intelligence workshops, and employee resource groups focused on diversity and inclusion. **"By prioritizing Emotional Intelligence, Google has created an environment where employees feel valued, supported, and empowered to bring their whole selves to work,"** Marvis explained. **"This culture of trust and inclusivity fosters creativity, teamwork, and resilience, driving innovation and success across the organization."**

A hand went up in the front row. **"How does Microsoft leverage EQ to drive organizational success?"**

Marvis nodded, appreciating the question. **"An excellent question. Microsoft is another example of a company that prioritizes Emotional Intelligence in its culture and operations,"** she replied. **"The company emphasizes the importance of empathy, communication, and collaboration in its leadership development programs and team-building initiatives."**

She clicked to the next slide, which highlighted examples of initiatives at Microsoft that promote EQ, such as empathy training for managers, inclusive leadership workshops, and employee resource groups focused on mental health and well-being. "**By cultivating a culture of empathy and inclusion, Microsoft has created a workplace where employees feel valued, respected, and supported in their personal and professional growth,**" Marvis noted. "**This culture of empathy drives collaboration, innovation, and excellence, positioning Microsoft as a leader in the tech industry.**"

The screen transitioned to examples of initiatives at Zappos, known for its unique company culture centered around customer service and employee happiness. "**Zappos is renowned for its focus on Emotional Intelligence and its commitment to creating a positive and engaging work environment,**" Marvis explained. "**The company places a strong emphasis on building meaningful connections among employees and fostering a culture of trust, authenticity, and fun.**"

She clicked to the next slide, which showcased examples of initiatives at Zappos that promote EQ, such as emotional intelligence training for customer service representatives, team-building activities focused on empathy and communication, and a company-wide emphasis on work-life balance and well-being. "**By prioritizing Emotional Intelligence and employee happiness, Zappos has created a culture where employees feel inspired, motivated, and empowered to deliver exceptional customer service and drive business success,**" Marvis noted. "**This culture of positivity and connection sets Zappos apart as a leader in customer experience and employee satisfaction.**"

The final slide summarized the key takeaways from the case studies, emphasizing the transformative impact of EQ on organizational success and employee well-being. "**In summary, organizations that prioritize Emotional Intelligence create** cultures where employees thrive, innovation flourishes, and success is achieved," Marvis concluded. **"By learning from these case studies, we can glean valuable insights into how EQ drives excellence and fosters a positive work culture, inspiring us to prioritize Emotional Intelligence in our own organizations."**

She finished with a thought-provoking statement, her voice resonating with admiration and aspiration. **"As we continue to explore the interplay between IQ and EQ in the workplace, let's challenge ourselves to emulate the success of these organizations by prioritizing Emotional Intelligence and creating cultures where every individual can flourish and contribute to the organization's success."**

The room filled with a sense of admiration and inspiration, the audience clearly motivated and eager to apply the lessons learned from the case studies to enhance EQ in their own organizations. Dr. Marvis Carter smiled, knowing she had illuminated a path to success driven by Emotional Intelligence and organizational excellence.

9

Chapter 9: Education: Teaching for Both IQ and EQ

The Importance of Teaching Emotional Intelligence

In a bustling auditorium filled with educators and administrators, Dr. Marvis Carter embarked on a journey through the realm of education, emphasizing the importance of teaching Emotional Intelligence (EQ) alongside Intellectual Quotient (IQ). She knew that equipping students with both cognitive and emotional skills was essential for their holistic development and success in life.

"**Welcome to Chapter 9 of our exploration: Education - Teaching for Both IQ and EQ,**" Marvis began, her voice projecting with passion. "**Today, we delve into the significance of incorporating Emotional Intelligence into our educational systems, preparing students not only for academic achievement but also for personal and professional success.**"

She clicked the remote, and the screen displayed a quote:

CHAPTER 9: EDUCATION: TEACHING FOR BOTH IQ AND EQ

"Education is the most powerful weapon which you can use to change the world." **"Let's begin by understanding why teaching Emotional Intelligence is crucial in education,"** Marvis continued. **"EQ refers to our ability to recognize, understand, and manage emotions, and it plays a vital role in shaping students' social interactions, personal well-being, and future success."**

The next slide showcased examples of how EQ influences various aspects of students' lives, from academic performance to relationships and mental health. **"By teaching Emotional Intelligence, we empower students to navigate challenges, build positive relationships, and make responsible decisions,"** Marvis explained. **"These skills are essential not only for academic success but also for fostering resilience, empathy, and adaptability in an ever-changing world."**

A hand went up in the front row. **"How can educators incorporate EQ into their teaching practices?"**

Marvis nodded, appreciating the question. **"An excellent question. Educators can incorporate EQ into their teaching practices through a variety of strategies,"** she replied. **"This includes integrating social-emotional learning (SEL) programs into the curriculum, fostering a supportive and inclusive classroom environment, and providing opportunities for students to develop self-awareness, self-management, social awareness, relationship skills, and responsible decision-making."**

She clicked to the next slide, which highlighted examples of activities and initiatives that promote EQ in the classroom, such as mindfulness exercises, peer collaboration projects, conflict resolution workshops, and discussions on empathy and emotional regulation. **"By incorporating these** practices into their teaching, educators can create a learning environment that nurtures students' emotional intelligence alongside their academic skills," Marvis noted. "This holistic approach to education prepares students to succeed not only in school but also in life."

The screen transitioned to examples of schools and educational programs known for their emphasis on teaching Emotional Intelligence and fostering a positive school culture. "From elementary schools to universities, educational institutions around the world are recognizing the importance of teaching Emotional Intelligence," Marvis explained. "These schools prioritize SEL, character education, and mental health support to ensure that students receive a well-rounded education that prepares them for success in a rapidly changing society."

A hand went up in the middle row. "How can policymakers support the integration of EQ into education?"

Marvis considered the question thoughtfully. "Policymakers play a crucial role in supporting the integration of EQ into education by advocating for policies and funding initiatives that prioritize social-emotional learning, teacher training in EQ instruction, and research into best practices," she replied. "Additionally, fostering partnerships between schools, communities, and mental health organizations can provide additional resources and support for teaching Emotional Intelligence effectively."

The final slide summarized the key takeaways from the discussion, emphasizing the transformative impact of teaching Emotional Intelligence on students' academic achievement, personal development, and future success. "**In summary,** teaching Emotional Intelligence is essential for equipping students with the skills they need to thrive in school, in their careers, and in life," Marvis concluded. "By prioritizing EQ alongside IQ in education, we can empower students to become compassionate, resilient, and socially responsible individuals who contribute positively to their communities and society as a whole."

She finished with a thought-provoking statement, her voice resonating with hope and determination. "As we continue to explore the interplay between IQ and EQ in education, let's challenge ourselves to prioritize the holistic development of students, creating learning environments where every child can reach their full potential and make a positive impact on the world."

The auditorium filled with a sense of purpose and inspiration, the audience clearly motivated and eager to integrate Emotional Intelligence into their teaching practices and educational systems. Dr. Marvis Carter smiled, knowing she had ignited a spark that would transform education and empower future generations to thrive in a complex and ever-changing world.

Integrating EQ into the Curriculum

In the midst of a dynamic seminar hall filled with educators and administrators, Dr. Marvis Carter continued her exploration of the symbiotic relationship between Emotional Intelligence (EQ) and Intellectual Quotient (IQ) in education. As she delved deeper into the topic, she focused on the crucial aspect of integrating EQ into the curriculum, recognizing its transformative potential in shaping students' holistic development.

"**As we journey further into Chapter 9, let's delve into the vital task of integrating Emotional Intelligence into the curriculum,**" Marvis proclaimed, her voice resonating with purpose. "**By embedding EQ into our educational framework, we equip students with essential skills for navigating life's complexities with resilience and empathy.**"

She clicked the remote, and the screen illuminated with a quote: *"Education is not the filling of a pail, but the lighting of a fire."* "**Let's commence by understanding the significance of integrating EQ into the curriculum,**" Marvis continued. "**EQ encompasses a spectrum of skills, including self-awareness, social awareness, self-regulation, relationship management, and responsible decision-making. By weaving these skills into the curriculum, we empower students to thrive academically, socially, and emotionally.**"

The next slide showcased examples of how EQ could be seamlessly integrated into various subjects, from language arts to mathematics, science to social studies. "**By infusing EQ into the curriculum, educators foster an environment where students not only master academic content but also cultivate essential life skills,**" Marvis explained. "**For instance, in language arts, students may explore characters' emotions in literature, enhancing their empathy and understanding of human experiences. In mathematics, problem-solving activities may encourage teamwork and collaboration, promoting social awareness and relationship skills.**"

A hand went up in the front row. "**How can educators effectively integrate EQ into the curriculum without detracting from academic content?**"

Marvis nodded, acknowledging the query. "**An insightful question indeed. Effective integration of EQ into the curriculum involves aligning social-emotional learning objectives with academic standards and leveraging interdisciplinary approaches,**" she replied. "**For instance, educators can design project-based learning experiences that incorporate EQ skills while addressing academic content. Additionally, embedding mindfulness practices, cooperative learning activities, and reflection exercises into daily routines can seamlessly integrate EQ into the learning process.**"

She clicked to the next slide, which highlighted examples of EQ-integrated lesson plans and activities, ranging from journaling exercises to role-playing scenarios, from collaborative projects to community service initiatives. "**By fostering a culture of social-emotional learning in the classroom, educators create opportunities for students to develop essential EQ skills in authentic and meaningful contexts,**" Marvis noted. "**This holistic approach to education nurtures students' emotional intelligence alongside their academic growth, preparing them for success in school and beyond.**"

The screen transitioned to examples of schools and districts that have successfully integrated EQ into their curriculum, showcasing the positive impact on student achievement, engagement, and well-being. "**From elementary schools to high schools, educational institutions are recognizing the transformative power of integrating EQ into the curriculum,**" Marvis explained. "**These schools prioritize social-emotional learning as a foundational component of education, equipping students with the skills they need** to thrive in a complex and interconnected world."

A hand went up in the middle row. "**How can educators assess students' progress in developing EQ skills?**"

Marvis considered the question thoughtfully. "**Assessing EQ skills requires a multifaceted approach that goes beyond traditional measures of academic achievement,**" she replied. "**Educators can use a combination of self-assessments, peer evaluations, observation checklists, and performance tasks to gauge students' progress in developing EQ skills. Additionally, fostering a culture of reflection and feedback allows students to track their growth and set goals for further development.**"

The final slide summarized the key takeaways from the discussion, emphasizing the transformative impact of integrating EQ into the curriculum on students' holistic development and success. "**In summary, integrating EQ into the curriculum is essential for preparing students to thrive academically, socially, and emotionally,**" Marvis concluded. "**By infusing social-emotional learning into every aspect of education, we empower students to become compassionate, resilient, and socially responsible individuals who contribute positively to their communities and society.**"

She finished with a thought-provoking statement, her voice resonating with conviction and optimism. "**As we continue to explore the interplay between IQ and EQ in education, let's challenge ourselves to integrate social-emotional learning into the curriculum, lighting the path for students to become lifelong learners and compassionate leaders of tomorrow.**"

The seminar hall buzzed with excitement and inspiration, the audience invigorated and eager to embark on the journey of integrating EQ into their curriculum to nurture students' holistic development. Dr. Marvis Carter smiled, knowing she had ignited a spark that would illuminate the way forward for education.

Developing Intellectual Skills in Students

As the discussion in the seminar hall progressed, Dr. Marvis Carter shifted her focus to the complementary aspect of developing intellectual skills in students alongside Emotional Intelligence (EQ). Recognizing the importance of fostering cognitive abilities alongside social-emotional learning, she embarked on a journey to explore strategies for nurturing students' intellectual growth within the educational framework.

"Now, let's delve into the essential task of developing intellectual skills in students," Marvis declared, her voice infused with determination. **"In tandem with teaching Emotional Intelligence, it's imperative that we equip students with the cognitive abilities they need to succeed academically and thrive in a knowledge-driven world."**

She clicked the remote, and the screen displayed a quote: *"Education is the passport to the future, for tomorrow belongs to those who prepare for it today."* **"Let's begin by understanding the significance of developing intellectual skills in students,"** Marvis continued. **"Intellectual skills encompass a range of abilities, including critical thinking, problem-solving, creativity, and information literacy. By cultivating these skills, we empower students to analyze, innovate, and adapt to the complexities of the modern world."**

The next slide showcased examples of how educators can foster intellectual skills across various subjects, from mathematics to literature, science to history. "**By embedding opportunities for intellectual growth into the curriculum, educators ignite students' curiosity and fuel their passion for learning,**" Marvis explained. "**For instance, in mathematics, students may engage in problem-solving activities that require logical reasoning and mathematical fluency. In literature, they may explore complex themes and analyze literary devices to deepen their understanding of texts.**"

A hand went up in the front row. "**How can educators ensure that students develop a strong foundation in intellectual skills?**"

Marvis nodded, acknowledging the inquiry. "**An insightful question indeed. Developing a strong foundation in intellectual skills requires intentional planning, differentiated instruction, and authentic learning experiences,**" she replied. "**Educators can design lessons that encourage inquiry, exploration, and experimentation, allowing students to apply their knowledge and skills in real-world contexts. Additionally, providing opportunities for collaborative problem-solving and project-based learning fosters creativity, teamwork, and innovation.**"

She clicked to the next slide, which highlighted examples of lesson plans and activities that promote the development of intellectual skills, such as inquiry-based investigations, Socratic seminars, hands-on experiments, and design challenges. "**By engaging students in intellectually stimulating experiences, educators nurture their ability to think critically, communicate effectively, and collaborate with others,**" Marvis noted. "**This holistic approach to education prepares students to excel academically and become**

CHAPTER 9: EDUCATION: TEACHING FOR BOTH IQ AND EQ

lifelong learners who contribute meaningfully to society."

The screen transitioned to examples of schools and districts that prioritize the development of intellectual skills in their curriculum, showcasing the positive impact on student achievement, engagement, and future success. **"From elementary schools to high schools, educational institutions are recognizing the importance of fostering intellectual skills in students,"** Marvis explained. **"These schools prioritize inquiry-based learning, project-based assessments, and interdisciplinary approaches to education, empowering students to become critical thinkers, problem solvers, and innovators."**

A hand went up in the middle row. **"How can educators support students in developing intellectual skills across diverse learning styles and abilities?"**

Marvis considered the question thoughtfully. **"Supporting students in developing intellectual skills requires differentiation, scaffolding, and personalized learning experiences,"** she replied. **"Educators can provide a variety of instructional strategies, resources, and assessments to meet the diverse needs of students, fostering a culture of equity and inclusion in the classroom. Additionally, fostering a growth mindset and celebrating students' progress and achievements cultivates a positive learning environment where all students can thrive."**

The final slide summarized the key takeaways from the discussion, emphasizing the transformative impact of developing intellectual skills in students on their academic achievement, critical thinking, and future success. **"In summary, developing intellectual skills in students is essential for preparing them to succeed academically and thrive in a knowledge-**

driven world," Marvis concluded. "By fostering curiosity, creativity, and critical thinking, educators empower students to become lifelong learners who contribute positively to society and shape the future."

She finished with a thought-provoking statement, her voice resonating with conviction and optimism. **"As we continue to explore the interplay between IQ and EQ in education, let's challenge ourselves to cultivate a learning environment where students develop both their intellectual skills and emotional intelligence, preparing them to navigate the complexities of the modern world with confidence and resilience."**

The seminar hall buzzed with inspiration and determination, the audience invigorated and eager to embark on the journey of developing intellectual skills in their students. Dr. Marvis Carter smiled, knowing she had ignited a spark that would illuminate the path to academic excellence and lifelong learning.

Teaching Methods that Foster Both IQ and EQ

In the midst of an engaged audience of educators and administrators, Dr. Marvis Carter delved into the critical aspect of teaching methods that foster the development of both Intellectual Quotient (IQ) and Emotional Intelligence (EQ). Recognizing the interconnectedness of cognitive and emotional skills in students' holistic development, she embarked on a journey to explore strategies that seamlessly integrate both aspects within the educational framework.

"As we delve deeper into Chapter 9, let's explore the vital realm of teaching methods that foster the development of

both IQ and EQ," Marvis declared, her voice exuding passion and conviction. **"By adopting pedagogical approaches that nurture both cognitive and emotional skills, educators create a dynamic learning environment where students thrive academically and emotionally."**

She clicked the remote, and the screen illuminated with a quote: *"Education is not preparation for life; education is life itself."* **"Let's commence by understanding the significance of teaching methods that foster both IQ and EQ,"** Marvis continued. **"Effective teaching methods should not only facilitate the acquisition of knowledge and skills but also promote self-awareness, empathy, collaboration, and critical thinking."**

The next slide showcased examples of teaching methods that seamlessly integrate both IQ and EQ, such as project-based learning, inquiry-based instruction, cooperative learning, and social-emotional learning activities. **"By incorporating these methods into the classroom, educators create opportunities for students to develop cognitive and emotional skills in tandem,"** Marvis explained. **"For instance, in project-based learning, students engage in collaborative projects that require critical thinking, problem-solving, and communication skills, while also fostering empathy, teamwork, and self-management."**

A hand went up in the front row. **"How can educators ensure that teaching methods effectively foster both IQ and EQ?"**

Marvis nodded, acknowledging the inquiry. **"An insightful question indeed. Ensuring that teaching methods effectively foster both IQ and EQ requires intentional planning, alignment with learning objectives, and ongoing** assessment and reflection," she replied. "**Educators can design lessons that integrate cognitive and emotional skills by incorporating interdisciplinary approaches, authentic learning experiences, and opportunities for self-reflection and peer feedback.**"

She clicked to the next slide, which highlighted examples of teaching methods and activities that promote the development of both IQ and EQ, such as Socratic seminars, problem-based learning, role-playing scenarios, and reflective journals. "**By engaging students in intellectually stimulating and emotionally supportive learning experiences, educators create a culture of inquiry, empathy, and collaboration in the classroom,**" Marvis noted. "**This holistic approach to education prepares students to excel academically and thrive emotionally, equipping them with the skills they need to succeed in school and in life.**"

The screen transitioned to examples of classrooms and schools where teaching methods that foster both IQ and EQ are embraced, showcasing the positive impact on student engagement, achievement, and well-being. "**From elementary classrooms to high schools, educators are embracing teaching methods that nurture both cognitive and emotional skills in students,**" Marvis explained. "**These classrooms prioritize student-centered learning, collaboration, and inquiry, creating a supportive and empowering learning environment where every student can succeed.**"

A hand went up in the middle row. "**How can educators support students in developing both their cognitive and emotional skills?**"

Marvis considered the question thoughtfully. "**Supporting students in developing both their cognitive and emotional** skills requires fostering a culture of growth, resilience, and empathy in the classroom," she replied. "Educators can provide opportunities for students to practice self-awareness, self-regulation, and social awareness through mindfulness activities, cooperative learning experiences, and reflective discussions. Additionally, creating a safe and inclusive classroom climate where students feel valued, respected, and supported encourages risk-taking, creativity, and collaboration."

The final slide summarized the key takeaways from the discussion, emphasizing the transformative impact of teaching methods that foster both IQ and EQ on students' holistic development and success. "In summary, teaching methods that foster both IQ and EQ create a dynamic learning environment where students thrive academically and emotionally," Marvis concluded. "By integrating cognitive and emotional skills into the curriculum, educators empower students to become lifelong learners who contribute positively to their communities and society."

She finished with a thought-provoking statement, her voice resonating with conviction and optimism. "As we continue to explore the interplay between IQ and EQ in education, let's challenge ourselves to embrace teaching methods that foster both cognitive and emotional skills, lighting the path for students to become compassionate, resilient, and intellectually curious individuals who shape the future."

The seminar hall buzzed with inspiration and determination, the audience invigorated and eager to implement teaching methods that foster both IQ and EQ in their classrooms. Dr. Marvis Carter smiled, knowing she had ignited a spark that would transform education and empower future generations to thrive in a complex and ever-changing world.

Assessing Student Growth in IQ and EQ

In the midst of an engaged seminar hall filled with educators and administrators, Dr. Marvis Carter shifted the focus of the discussion to the critical aspect of assessing student growth in both Intellectual Quotient (IQ) and Emotional Intelligence (EQ). Recognizing the importance of measuring progress in cognitive and emotional skills, she embarked on a journey to explore strategies for evaluating students' holistic development within the educational framework.

"As we continue our exploration in Chapter 9, let's delve into the essential task of assessing student growth in both IQ and EQ," Marvis announced, her voice resonating with purpose and determination. **"By adopting comprehensive assessment practices, educators gain valuable insights into students' academic achievement, critical thinking, and social-emotional well-being."**

She clicked the remote, and the screen illuminated with a quote: *"Assessment should be a journey of discovery, not a series of hurdles."* **"Let's commence by understanding the significance of assessing student growth in both IQ and EQ,"** Marvis continued. **"Effective assessment practices not only measure academic proficiency but also evaluate students' ability to think critically, communicate effectively, and collaborate with others."**

The next slide showcased examples of assessment methods that encompass both IQ and EQ, such as performance tasks, portfolios, self-assessments, and social-emotional check-ins.

"By incorporating these methods into the assessment framework, educators gain a holistic understanding of students' strengths, challenges, and growth areas," Marvis explained. "For instance, performance tasks allow students to demonstrate their problem-solving skills and creativity, while self-assessments provide opportunities for reflection and goal-setting."

A hand went up in the front row. "How can educators ensure that assessment practices effectively measure both IQ and EQ?"

Marvis nodded, acknowledging the inquiry. "An insightful question indeed. Ensuring that assessment practices effectively measure both IQ and EQ requires alignment with learning objectives, differentiation to meet diverse needs, and ongoing feedback and reflection," she replied. "Educators can design assessments that integrate cognitive and emotional skills by incorporating a variety of methods, such as project-based assessments, peer evaluations, and rubrics that assess both academic and social-emotional competencies."

She clicked to the next slide, which highlighted examples of assessment tools and practices that promote the evaluation of both IQ and EQ, such as performance rubrics with criteria for critical thinking and collaboration, student-led conferences where students reflect on their academic and social-emotional growth, and portfolio assessments that showcase students' academic work alongside reflections on their learning journey. "By engaging students in the assessment process and providing opportunities for self-reflection and peer feedback, educators empower students to take ownership of their learning and growth," Marvis noted. "This holistic approach to assessment fosters a culture of continuous improvement and supports students' development of both cognitive and emotional skills."

The screen transitioned to examples of schools and districts where assessment practices that measure both IQ and EQ are embraced, showcasing the positive impact on student engagement, motivation, and achievement. "**From elementary classrooms to high schools, educators are embracing assessment practices that evaluate both cognitive and emotional skills in students,**" Marvis explained. "**These schools prioritize formative assessment, student-centered feedback, and growth-oriented assessment practices, creating a supportive and empowering learning environment where every student can succeed.**"

A hand went up in the middle row. "**How can educators use assessment data to inform instructional practices and support student growth in both IQ and EQ?**"

Marvis considered the question thoughtfully. "**Using assessment data to inform instructional practices and support student growth in both IQ and EQ requires data-driven decision-making, targeted interventions, and ongoing communication with students and families,**" she replied. "**Educators can analyze assessment data to identify areas of strength and growth for individual students, tailor instruction to meet diverse needs, and provide differentiated support and enrichment opportunities. Additionally, fostering a culture of feedback and reflection allows students to set goals, track their progress, and take ownership of their learning journey.**"

The final slide summarized the key takeaways from the discussion, emphasizing the importance of comprehensive assessment practices in evaluating students' holistic development and guiding instructional decision-making. **"In summary, assessing student growth in both IQ and EQ is essential for supporting their holistic development and success,"** Marvis concluded. **"By integrating cognitive and emotional assessments into the evaluation framework, educators empower students to become self-directed learners who thrive academically and emotionally."**

She finished with a thought-provoking statement, her voice resonating with conviction and optimism. **"As we continue to explore the interplay between IQ and EQ in education, let's challenge ourselves to embrace assessment practices that measure both cognitive and emotional skills, guiding students on a journey of discovery and growth."**

The seminar hall buzzed with inspiration and determination, the audience invigorated and eager to implement comprehensive assessment practices that measure both IQ and EQ in their classrooms. Dr. Marvis Carter smiled, knowing she had ignited a spark that would illuminate the path to student success and holistic development.

Preparing Students for a Balanced Future

In the heart of a vibrant seminar hall, Dr. Marvis Carter approached the culmination of Chapter 9 with a focus on preparing students for a balanced future. Understanding the interconnectedness of Intellectual Quotient (IQ) and Emotional Intelligence (EQ) in shaping students' holistic development, she embarked on a final exploration of strategies to equip them for success in a complex and ever-changing world.

"As we near the conclusion of Chapter 9, let's delve

into the crucial task of preparing students for a balanced future," Marvis declared, her voice resonating with urgency and hope. "By fostering both cognitive and emotional skills, educators lay the foundation for students to thrive academically, socially, and emotionally in the years to come."

She clicked the remote, and the screen illuminated with a quote: *"The future belongs to those who prepare for it today."* "Let's begin by understanding the significance of preparing students for a balanced future," Marvis continued. "In today's rapidly evolving world, success requires more than just academic knowledge—it demands resilience, adaptability, empathy, and innovation. By cultivating both IQ and EQ, educators empower students to navigate the complexities of the future with confidence and purpose."

The next slide showcased examples of strategies and initiatives that prepare students for a balanced future, such as interdisciplinary learning experiences, career readiness programs, leadership development opportunities, and social-emotional support services. "By integrating these strategies into the educational framework, educators create a dynamic learning environment that equips students with the skills they need to succeed in a diverse and interconnected world," Marvis explained. "For instance, career readiness programs help students explore their interests, talents, and aspirations, while leadership development opportunities foster confidence, communication, and collaboration skills."

A hand went up in the front row. "How can educators ensure that students are prepared for the challenges and opportunities of the future?"

CHAPTER 9: EDUCATION: TEACHING FOR BOTH IQ AND EQ

Marvis nodded, appreciating the question. **"An excellent question indeed. Ensuring that students are prepared for the challenges and opportunities of the future requires a multifaceted approach that integrates academic rigor, social-emotional support, and real-world experiences,"** she replied. **"Educators can provide opportunities for students to apply their knowledge and skills in authentic contexts, engage with diverse perspectives, and develop a sense of purpose and responsibility as global citizens."**

She clicked to the next slide, which highlighted examples of schools and districts that prioritize preparing students for a balanced future, showcasing the positive impact on student engagement, achievement, and post-graduation success. **"From elementary classrooms to high schools, educational institutions are embracing innovative approaches to prepare students for the future,"** Marvis explained. **"These schools prioritize holistic development, personalized learning, and partnerships with businesses and community organizations, ensuring that students graduate with the skills and mindset they need to thrive in college, career, and life."**

A hand went up in the middle row. **"How can educators foster a culture of lifelong learning and growth mindset in students?"**

Marvis considered the question thoughtfully. **"Fostering a culture of lifelong learning and growth mindset in students requires modeling curiosity, resilience, and a commitment to continuous improvement,"** she replied. "Educators can create opportunities for students to explore new ideas, take risks, and learn from failure. Additionally, providing feedback that focuses on effort, progress, and strategies encourages students to embrace challenges and persist in the face of obstacles."

The final slide summarized the key takeaways from the discussion, emphasizing the importance of preparing students for a balanced future by fostering both cognitive and emotional skills. **"In summary, preparing students for a balanced future requires a holistic approach to education that integrates both IQ and EQ,"** Marvis concluded. **"By equipping students with the knowledge, skills, and mindset they need to thrive in a complex and ever-changing world, educators empower them to become lifelong learners and compassionate leaders who shape the future."**

She finished with a thought-provoking statement, her voice resonating with conviction and optimism. **"As we conclude our exploration of Chapter 9, let's challenge ourselves to continue fostering both cognitive and emotional skills in students, preparing them not only for academic success but also for a life of purpose, fulfillment, and contribution to society."**

The seminar hall buzzed with inspiration and determination, the audience invigorated and eager to implement strategies that prepare students for a balanced future in their classrooms and schools. Dr. Marvis Carter smiled, knowing she had ignited a spark that would illuminate the path to student success and holistic development in the years to come.

10

Chapter 10: Cultivating Synergy: Practical Applications

Strategies for Enhancing Both IQ and EQ

In the final chapter of her seminar series, Dr. Marvis Carter shifted the focus to practical applications, exploring strategies for cultivating synergy between Intellectual Quotient (IQ) and Emotional Intelligence (EQ). Recognizing the transformative potential of integrating both cognitive and emotional skills, she embarked on a journey to provide educators with actionable insights to empower their students for success.

"As we embark on Chapter 10, let's explore practical strategies for enhancing both IQ and EQ," Marvis declared, her voice resonating with enthusiasm and determination. "**By leveraging synergies between cognitive and emotional skills, educators can create a learning environment where students thrive academically, socially, and emotionally.**"

She clicked the remote, and the screen illuminated with a

quote: *"The whole is greater than the sum of its parts."* **"Let's begin by understanding the significance of strategies that enhance both IQ and EQ,"** Marvis continued. **"These strategies go beyond traditional approaches to education, emphasizing the interconnectedness of cognitive and emotional development in students' holistic growth."**

The next slide showcased examples of practical strategies for enhancing both IQ and EQ, such as interdisciplinary projects, social-emotional learning activities, mindfulness practices, and reflective exercises. **"By incorporating these strategies into the classroom, educators create opportunities for students to develop cognitive and emotional skills in tandem,"** Marvis explained. **"For instance, interdisciplinary projects allow students to apply their academic knowledge while collaborating with peers, fostering critical thinking, communication, and teamwork skills."**

A hand went up in the front row. **"How can educators effectively integrate these strategies into their teaching practices?"**

Marvis nodded, appreciating the question. **"An excellent question indeed. Effectively integrating these strategies into teaching practices requires intentional planning, collaboration, and ongoing reflection,"** she replied. **"Educators can design lessons that integrate cognitive and emotional skills by incorporating project-based learning, cooperative group work, and explicit instruction in social-emotional competencies. Additionally, fostering a supportive and inclusive classroom climate encourages risk-taking, empathy, and resilience in students."**

She clicked to the next slide, which highlighted examples of classrooms and schools that embrace practical strategies for enhancing both IQ and EQ, showcasing the positive impact on student engagement, motivation, and achievement. "**From elementary classrooms to high schools, educators are embracing innovative approaches to cultivate synergy between cognitive and emotional development,**" Marvis explained. "**These classrooms prioritize holistic growth, personalized learning, and student-centered instruction, creating a dynamic learning environment where every student can succeed.**"

A hand went up in the middle row. "**How can educators assess the effectiveness of these strategies in enhancing both IQ and EQ?**"

Marvis considered the question thoughtfully. "**Assessing the effectiveness of these strategies requires a combination of qualitative and quantitative measures, including student performance data, observation, self-assessment, and feedback,**" she replied. "**Educators can collect evidence of student growth in cognitive and emotional skills through formative and summative assessments, student reflections, and portfolio reviews. Additionally, soliciting feedback from students and families provides valuable insights into the impact of these strategies on student learning and well-being.**"

The final slide summarized the key takeaways from the discussion, emphasizing the importance of practical strategies for enhancing both IQ and EQ in students. "**In summary, cultivating synergy between cognitive and emotional development requires intentional planning, collaboration, and ongoing assessment,**" Marvis concluded. "**By embracing these strategies, educators empower students to thrive academically, socially, and emotionally, preparing them

for success in school and beyond."

She finished with a thought-provoking statement, her voice resonating with conviction and optimism. **"As we conclude our exploration of Chapter 10, let's challenge ourselves to continue cultivating synergy between IQ and EQ in our teaching practices, empowering students to reach their full potential as lifelong learners and compassionate leaders."**

The seminar hall buzzed with inspiration and determination, the audience invigorated and eager to implement practical strategies for enhancing both IQ and EQ in their classrooms. Dr. Marvis Carter smiled, knowing she had ignited a spark that would illuminate the path to student success and holistic development.

Exercises and Activities for Balanced Development

As Dr. Marvis Carter delved deeper into Chapter 10, she turned her attention to practical exercises and activities aimed at fostering balanced development between Intellectual Quotient (IQ) and Emotional Intelligence (EQ). Recognizing the importance of hands-on experiences in nurturing both cognitive and emotional skills, she embarked on a journey to provide educators with actionable tools to empower their students.

"Now, let's explore exercises and activities for balanced development," Marvis declared, her voice infused with energy and purpose. **"By engaging students in meaningful experiences that integrate both IQ and EQ, educators can cultivate a holistic approach to learning and growth."**

She clicked the remote, and the screen displayed a quote: *"Education is not the filling of a pail, but the lighting of a fire."* **"Let's** begin by understanding the significance of exercises and activities that promote balanced development," Marvis continued. "These activities go beyond rote learning, encouraging students to explore, inquire, and reflect on both academic content and emotional experiences."

The next slide showcased examples of exercises and activities for balanced development, such as:

1. **Mindfulness Meditation:** Guided meditation sessions to promote self-awareness, focus, and emotional regulation.
2. **Journaling Prompts:** Reflective writing exercises to encourage self-expression, introspection, and empathy.
3. **Team-building Challenges:** Collaborative tasks and games to foster communication, problem-solving, and social-emotional skills.
4. **Debate and Discussion:** Structured debates and discussions to develop critical thinking, argumentation, and perspective-taking abilities.

"**By incorporating these exercises and activities into the classroom, educators create opportunities for students to engage both their minds and hearts,**" Marvis explained. "**For instance, mindfulness meditation helps students develop self-awareness and emotional regulation, while journaling prompts encourage reflection and empathy.**"

A hand went up in the front row. "**How can educators ensure that these exercises and activities are effectively integrated into the curriculum?**"

Marvis nodded, acknowledging the inquiry. "**An excellent question indeed. Effectively integrating these exercises** and activities requires alignment with learning objectives, differentiation to meet diverse needs, and ongoing reflection and adjustment," she replied. "Educators can embed these activities into lesson plans, incorporate them into daily routines, and provide opportunities for student choice and autonomy. Additionally, fostering a supportive and inclusive classroom environment encourages participation and engagement in these activities."

She clicked to the next slide, which highlighted examples of classrooms and schools that embrace exercises and activities for balanced development, showcasing the positive impact on student engagement, motivation, and well-being. "**From elementary classrooms to high schools, educators are embracing innovative approaches to cultivate balanced development in students,**" Marvis explained. "**These classrooms prioritize holistic growth, experiential learning, and social-emotional support, creating a dynamic and nurturing environment where every student can thrive.**"

A hand went up in the middle row. "**How can educators assess the effectiveness of these exercises and activities in promoting balanced development?**"

Marvis considered the question thoughtfully. "**Assessing the effectiveness of these exercises and activities requires a combination of observation, student feedback, and analysis of outcomes,**" she replied. "**Educators can observe student participation and engagement during activities, solicit feedback through surveys or discussions, and analyze changes in student behavior and attitudes over time. Additionally, monitoring academic and social-emotional growth through formative and summative assessments provides valuable insights into the impact of** these activities on student development."

The final slide summarized the key takeaways from the discussion, emphasizing the importance of exercises and activities for promoting balanced development between IQ and EQ. **"In summary, incorporating exercises and activities that engage both the mind and heart empowers students to develop a holistic approach to learning and growth,"** Marvis concluded. **"By embracing these tools, educators create a supportive and enriching environment where students thrive academically, socially, and emotionally."**

She finished with a thought-provoking statement, her voice resonating with conviction and optimism. **"As we conclude our exploration of Chapter 10, let's challenge ourselves to continue integrating exercises and activities for balanced development into our teaching practices, nurturing the minds and hearts of our students as they embark on their journey of lifelong learning and growth."**

The seminar hall buzzed with inspiration and determination, the audience invigorated and eager to implement practical tools for promoting balanced development in their classrooms. Dr. Marvis Carter smiled, knowing she had ignited a spark that would illuminate the path to student success and holistic development.

Building Emotional and Intellectual Resilience

As Dr. Marvis Carter continued to unravel the practical applications in Chapter 10, she pivoted the spotlight onto the critical aspect of building emotional and intellectual resilience. Recognizing the indispensable role of resilience in navigating the complexities of life, she embarked on a journey to equip educators with tangible strategies to foster resilience in their students.

"**Now, let's explore how to build emotional and intellectual resilience,**" Marvis proclaimed, her voice resonating with unwavering determination. "**By nurturing resilience, educators empower students to overcome challenges, persevere in the face of adversity, and thrive in an ever-changing world.**"

She clicked the remote, and the screen illuminated with a quote: *"Strength does not come from winning. Your struggles develop your strengths."* "**Let's commence by understanding the significance of building emotional and intellectual resilience,**" Marvis continued. "**Resilience equips students with the skills and mindset to bounce back from setbacks, learn from failures, and adapt to new situations.**"

The next slide showcased examples of strategies for building emotional and intellectual resilience, such as:

1. **Growth Mindset:** Encouraging a belief in the power of effort and persistence to overcome challenges and achieve goals.
2. **Coping Skills Training:** Teaching students effective strategies for managing stress, regulating emotions, and seeking support.
3. **Failure as Learning Opportunity:** Embracing failure as a natural part of the learning process and encouraging reflection and growth.
4. **Positive Affirmations:** Promoting self-confidence and self-belief through affirmations and positive self-talk.

"**By incorporating these strategies into the classroom,**

educators create a supportive environment where students feel empowered to face challenges with confidence and resilience," Marvis explained. "For instance, fostering a growth mindset helps students view setbacks as opportunities for growth, while coping skills training equips them with effective strategies to navigate stress and adversity."

A hand went up in the front row. "**How can educators ensure that these strategies are effectively implemented and sustained over time?**"

Marvis nodded, acknowledging the inquiry. "**An excellent question indeed. Ensuring the effective implementation and sustainability of these strategies requires ongoing support, modeling, and reinforcement,**" she replied. "**Educators can provide consistent messaging about the importance of resilience, model resilient behaviors, and integrate resilience-building activities into the curriculum. Additionally, creating a culture of support and collaboration encourages students to seek help when needed and reinforces the importance of resilience in achieving success.**"

She clicked to the next slide, which highlighted examples of classrooms and schools that prioritize building emotional and intellectual resilience, showcasing the positive impact on student well-being, academic achievement, and post-graduation success. "**From elementary classrooms to high schools, educators are embracing strategies to cultivate resilience in students,**" Marvis explained. "**These classrooms prioritize social-emotional learning, mental health support, and positive reinforcement, creating a nurturing environment where every student can thrive.**"

A hand went up in the middle row. "**How can educators help students develop resilience in the face of academic challenges?**"

Marvis considered the question thoughtfully. "**Helping students develop resilience in the face of academic challenges requires providing opportunities for growth, support, and reflection,**" she replied. "**Educators can scaffold assignments and tasks to ensure they are challenging yet achievable, provide constructive feedback that focuses on effort and improvement, and offer opportunities for students to reflect on their learning process and set goals for the future. Additionally, fostering a growth mindset and a sense of belonging in the classroom empowers students to persevere in the face of academic challenges.**"

The final slide summarized the key takeaways from the discussion, emphasizing the importance of building emotional and intellectual resilience in students. "**In summary, fostering resilience empowers students to navigate challenges with confidence and adaptability,**" Marvis concluded. "**By embracing strategies to build emotional and intellectual resilience, educators create a supportive and empowering environment where every student can reach their full potential.**"

She finished with a thought-provoking statement, her voice resonating with conviction and optimism. "**As we conclude our exploration of Chapter 10, let's challenge ourselves to continue fostering resilience in our students, equipping them with the tools and mindset to thrive in school and beyond.**"

The seminar hall buzzed with inspiration and determination, the audience invigorated and eager to implement practical strategies for building emotional and intellectual resilience in their classrooms. Dr. Marvis Carter smiled, knowing she had ignited a spark that would illuminate the path to student success and well-being.

Real-Life Applications and Success Stories

As Dr. Marvis Carter delved deeper into Chapter 10, she shifted the focus onto real-life applications and success stories, aiming to inspire educators with tangible examples of how the integration of Intellectual Quotient (IQ) and Emotional Intelligence (EQ) can lead to meaningful outcomes in students' lives. Recognizing the power of storytelling in driving home key concepts, she embarked on a journey to showcase the transformative impact of balanced development.

"Now, let's explore real-life applications and success stories," Marvis declared, her voice imbued with a sense of excitement and possibility. "By learning from the experiences of others, educators can gain valuable insights into how the integration of IQ and EQ can shape students' paths to success."

She clicked the remote, and the screen illuminated with a quote: *"The future belongs to those who believe in the beauty of their dreams."* "Let's begin by understanding the significance of real-life applications and success stories," Marvis continued. "These stories serve as powerful examples of how the cultivation of both cognitive and emotional skills can empower students to achieve their dreams and make a positive impact in the world."

The next slide showcased examples of real-life applications and success stories, such as:

1. **Social Entrepreneurship:** Students who use their creativity and empathy to address social and environmental challenges through innovative projects and ventures.
2. **Leadership and Advocacy:** Young leaders who leverage their communication and collaboration skills to advocate for positive change in their communities.
3. **Academic Achievement:** Students who excel academically while demonstrating resilience, grit, and a growth mindset in the face of challenges.
4. **Personal Growth:** Individuals who overcome adversity, cultivate self-awareness, and develop strong interpersonal relationships through their journey of self-discovery.

"**By highlighting these real-life examples, educators can inspire students to believe in their own potential and pursue their passions with confidence and determination,**" Marvis explained. "**For instance, showcasing social entrepreneurship projects encourages students to think creatively and compassionately about how they can make a difference in the world, while celebrating academic achievement reinforces the importance of resilience and perseverance in reaching one's goals.**"

A hand went up in the front row. "**How can educators incorporate these real-life applications and success stories into their teaching practices?**"

Marvis nodded, acknowledging the inquiry. "**An excellent question indeed. Incorporating these stories into teaching practices requires intentional planning, relevance, and authenticity,**" she replied. "**Educators can share stories of real-life applications and success stories during lessons,** integrate them into curriculum units, and invite guest speakers or alumni to share their experiences with students. Additionally, providing opportunities for students to reflect on and discuss these stories fosters deeper engagement and connection with the material."

She clicked to the next slide, which highlighted examples of classrooms and schools that embrace real-life applications and success stories, showcasing the positive impact on student motivation, engagement, and sense of purpose. "**From elementary classrooms to high schools, educators are harnessing the power of real-life examples to inspire and empower students,**" Marvis explained. "**These classrooms prioritize experiential learning, community engagement, and student-driven projects, creating a dynamic and meaningful learning environment where every student can thrive.**"

A hand went up in the middle row. "**How can educators measure the impact of these real-life applications and success stories on student outcomes?**"

Marvis considered the question thoughtfully. "**Measuring the impact of these stories on student outcomes requires a combination of qualitative and quantitative data, including student reflections, surveys, and academic performance indicators,**" she replied. "**Educators can assess changes in student motivation, engagement, and self-efficacy following exposure to real-life examples, as well as track academic progress and achievement over time. Additionally, soliciting feedback from students and families provides valuable insights into the perceived impact of these stories on student learning and development.**"

The final slide summarized the key takeaways from the discussion, emphasizing the importance of incorporating real-life applications and success stories into teaching practices. **"In summary, real-life examples inspire students to believe in their own potential and take meaningful action to pursue their dreams,"** Marvis concluded. **"By harnessing the power of storytelling, educators empower students to see themselves as agents of change and creators of their own destinies."**

She finished with a thought-provoking statement, her voice resonating with conviction and optimism. **"As we conclude our exploration of Chapter 10, let's challenge ourselves to continue sharing real-life applications and success stories with our students, igniting their passion and fueling their drive to make a positive impact in the world."**

The seminar hall buzzed with inspiration and determination, the audience invigorated and eager to incorporate real-life examples into their teaching practices. Dr. Marvis Carter smiled, knowing she had ignited a spark that would illuminate the path to student success and fulfillment.

Tools and Resources for Continued Growth

In the culmination of Chapter 10, Dr. Marvis Carter shifted the focus to tools and resources for continued growth, aiming to equip educators with the necessary support and guidance to sustain their efforts in integrating Intellectual Quotient (IQ) and Emotional Intelligence (EQ) in their teaching practices. Recognizing the importance of ongoing professional development, she embarked on a journey to provide educators with actionable tools and valuable resources to fuel their journey of growth.

"Now, let's explore tools and resources for continued growth," Marvis declared, her voice brimming with enthusiasm and dedication. **"By providing educators with the support they need, we ensure that the integration of IQ and EQ remains a cornerstone of their teaching practices, fostering a culture of lifelong learning and continuous improvement."**

She clicked the remote, and the screen illuminated with a quote: *"Education is not the filling of a pail, but the lighting of a fire."* **"Let's begin by understanding the significance of tools and resources for continued growth,"** Marvis continued. **"These resources serve as invaluable companions on the journey of professional development, offering insights, strategies, and inspiration to educators as they navigate the complexities of teaching and learning."**

The next slide showcased examples of tools and resources for continued growth, such as:

1. **Professional Development Workshops:** Opportunities for educators to participate in workshops, conferences, and seminars focused on topics related to IQ and EQ integration.
2. **Online Courses and Webinars:** Accessible and flexible learning opportunities that allow educators to deepen their knowledge and skills from the comfort of their own homes.
3. **Books and Articles:** Rich sources of information and inspiration, offering insights from experts in the fields of education, psychology, and leadership.
4. **Community of Practice:** Collaborative networks and

online communities where educators can connect with peers, share best practices, and seek advice and support.

"**By leveraging these tools and resources, educators can continue to refine their practice, explore new ideas, and stay abreast of the latest research and developments in the field,**" Marvis explained. "**For instance, participating in professional development workshops provides educators with hands-on experiences and practical strategies for integrating IQ and EQ into their teaching practices, while online courses and webinars offer convenient opportunities to deepen their understanding of key concepts and techniques.**"

A hand went up in the front row. "**How can educators navigate the vast array of tools and resources available to them?**"

Marvis nodded, acknowledging the inquiry. "**An excellent question indeed. Navigating the landscape of tools and resources requires intentionality, discernment, and a focus on personal and professional goals,**" she replied. "**Educators can start by identifying their areas of interest and areas for growth, then seek out resources that align with their needs and preferences. Additionally, cultivating a network of support, both online and offline, allows educators to share recommendations, seek advice, and collaborate with peers on their journey of growth.**"

She clicked to the next slide, which highlighted examples of educators who have benefited from tools and resources for continued growth, showcasing the positive impact on their teaching practices, student outcomes, and personal fulfillment. "**From novice teachers to seasoned educators, individuals** across the globe are leveraging tools and resources for continued growth," Marvis explained. "These educators prioritize their own development as learners and leaders, recognizing that their ongoing growth is essential to the success and well-being of their students."

A hand went up in the middle row. "How can educators ensure that they are making the most of these tools and resources?"

Marvis considered the question thoughtfully. "Making the most of these tools and resources requires a commitment to reflection, experimentation, and collaboration," she replied. "Educators can set aside time for regular reflection on their practice, experiment with new ideas and techniques, and seek feedback from colleagues and students. Additionally, staying curious and open-minded allows educators to remain responsive to the needs of their students and the evolving landscape of education."

The final slide summarized the key takeaways from the discussion, emphasizing the importance of tools and resources for continued growth in educators. "In summary, investing in tools and resources for continued growth empowers educators to cultivate their practice, inspire their students, and make a lasting impact in the field of education," Marvis concluded. "By embracing these resources, educators embark on a journey of lifelong learning and professional fulfillment, enriching their own lives and the lives of those they serve."

She finished with a thought-provoking statement, her voice resonating with conviction and optimism. "As we conclude our exploration of Chapter 10, let's challenge ourselves to continue seeking out tools and resources for continued

growth, empowering ourselves and our students to reach new heights of achievement and fulfillment."

The seminar hall buzzed with inspiration and determination, the audience invigorated and eager to explore the myriad tools and resources available to support their journey of growth. Dr. Marvis Carter smiled, knowing she had provided educators with the tools and inspiration they needed to cultivate synergy between IQ and EQ in their teaching practices, fostering a culture of excellence and innovation in education.

The Future of Intelligence: Embracing the Synergy

As Dr. Marvis Carter drew Chapter 10 to its climax, she cast her gaze towards the horizon, envisioning the future of intelligence and the pivotal role of synergy between Intellectual Quotient (IQ) and Emotional Intelligence (EQ). Recognizing the transformative potential of this integration in shaping the landscape of education and beyond, she embarked on a journey to inspire educators with a vision of possibility and progress.

"And now, let's turn our gaze towards the future of intelligence, where the synergy between IQ and EQ will illuminate the path forward," Marvis proclaimed, her voice resounding with a sense of purpose and anticipation. **"By embracing this synergy, we unlock new possibilities for learning, growth, and human flourishing."**

She clicked the remote, and the screen lit up with a quote: *"The future belongs to those who prepare for it today."* **"Let us begin by understanding the significance of embracing the synergy between IQ and EQ,"** Marvis continued. **"In a world characterized by rapid change and complexity, individuals who possess both cognitive and emotional** skills will be best equipped to navigate the challenges and seize the opportunities of tomorrow."

The next slide showcased glimpses of the future, where the integration of IQ and EQ permeated every aspect of society:

1. **Education:** Curricula that prioritize the development of both cognitive and emotional skills, preparing students to thrive in a dynamic and interconnected world.
2. **Workplace:** Organizations that value and cultivate a diverse range of intelligences, fostering innovation, collaboration, and resilience among employees.
3. **Leadership:** Leaders who lead with empathy, wisdom, and vision, inspiring others to reach their full potential and achieve collective goals.
4. **Global Challenges:** Solutions to pressing global challenges that emerge from a synthesis of intellectual rigor and emotional insight, driven by a commitment to social responsibility and sustainability.

"**By embracing the synergy between IQ and EQ, we pave the way for a future where intelligence is not defined by one's ability to solve equations or recall facts, but by one's capacity for empathy, creativity, and resilience,**" Marvis explained. "**In this future, individuals are empowered to lead meaningful lives, build thriving communities, and contribute to the greater good of humanity.**"

A hand went up in the front row. "**How can we, as educators, prepare our students for this future?**"

Marvis nodded, acknowledging the question. "**An excellent question indeed. As educators, our role is to nurture the seeds of potential within each of our students, equipping** them with the skills, knowledge, and mindset they need to thrive in the world of tomorrow," she replied. "We can do this by fostering a culture of curiosity, creativity, and compassion in our classrooms, by providing opportunities for students to engage in interdisciplinary learning, collaborative problem-solving, and real-world application of their skills."

She clicked to the next slide, which depicted a future where the synergy between IQ and EQ was the driving force behind progress and innovation. "In this future, the boundaries between disciplines blur, and the lines between intellect and emotion fade," Marvis explained. "It is a future where individuals embrace their uniqueness, celebrate diversity, and work together towards a common purpose."

A hand went up in the middle row. "What role do educators play in shaping this future?"

Marvis considered the question thoughtfully. "Educators play a central role in shaping the future of intelligence by cultivating a learning environment that values and nurtures both cognitive and emotional development," she replied. "We must lead by example, demonstrating empathy, resilience, and a commitment to lifelong learning. We must empower our students to think critically, communicate effectively, and collaborate with others. And we must instill in them a sense of purpose and agency, inspiring them to use their intelligence to make a positive impact in the world."

The final slide summarized the key takeaways from the discussion, emphasizing the importance of embracing the synergy between IQ and EQ in shaping the future of intelligence. "In summary, the future belongs to those who

CHAPTER 10: CULTIVATING SYNERGY: PRACTICAL APPLICATIONS

embrace the synergy between IQ and EQ, who recognize that true intelligence encompasses both cognitive and emotional skills," Marvis concluded. "As educators, let us embark on this journey together, preparing our students not only for the challenges of tomorrow but also for the opportunities to create a brighter, more compassionate, and more equitable world."

She finished with a thought-provoking statement, her voice resonating with conviction and hope. "As we conclude our exploration of Chapter 10, let us embrace the synergy between IQ and EQ, knowing that it holds the key to a future where intelligence is not just measured by what we know, but by who we are and how we impact the world around us."

The seminar hall buzzed with anticipation and excitement, the audience inspired and energized by the vision of a future where the integration of IQ and EQ leads to greater understanding, empathy, and innovation. Dr. Marvis Carter smiled, knowing that she had ignited a spark that would illuminate the path to a brighter tomorrow.

About the Author

Goodson Mumba is a multifaceted individual known for his diverse expertise and prolific contributions across various fields. As an infopreneur, thought leader, and spiritual leader, he has inspired countless individuals through his insightful teachings and impactful writings. Mumba is also an accomplished author, with several notable works to his name, including "Understanding Corporate Worship," "The Years I Spent in a Week," "Management By Harmony," "The CEO's Diary," "Change to Change" and "Creative Thinking for results" His literary works span topics ranging from business management to personal development and spirituality, reflecting his broad range of interests and insights.

With a Master of Business Leadership (MBL) and a Bachelor of Arts in Theology (BTh), Mumba brings a unique blend of business acumen and spiritual wisdom to his work. His educational background is further enriched by a Group Diploma in Management Studies, providing him with a solid foundation in organizational dynamics and leadership principles. Additionally, Mumba holds diplomas in Education Psychology, Leadership and Management Styles, Organizational Behaviour, Financial Accounting, Economic Growth and Development, and Project Management, showcasing his commitment to continuous learning and professional development.

Mumba's expertise extends beyond traditional academic disciplines, encompassing areas such as Neuro-Linguistic Programming (NLP) and Positive Psychology. His diverse skill set is complemented by a range of certifications, including Creative Problem Solving and Decision Making, Life Coaching Fundamentals and Techniques, Professional Life Coaching, and Performance Management System Design. These certifications reflect Mumba's dedication to equipping himself with the tools and knowledge necessary to empower others and drive positive change.

As an author, Mumba's writings reflect his deep understanding of human nature, organizational dynamics, and spiritual principles. His works offer practical insights, actionable strategies, and inspirational guidance for individuals seeking personal growth, professional success, and spiritual fulfillment. Mumba's holistic approach to life and leadership resonates with readers worldwide, making him a respected figure in both the business and spiritual communities.

Overall, Goodson Mumba's diverse background, extensive knowledge, and profound insights make him a sought-after speaker, mentor, and author. His commitment to excellence, lifelong learning, and service to others continues to inspire individuals to unlock their full potential and lead lives of purpose and significance.

Goodson Mumba is renowned for initiating the concept of Management by Harmony, revolutionizing traditional management practices with a focus on balanced and holistic approaches. He has authored two influential books on this subject: "Introduction to Management by Harmony" and its sequel, "Management by Harmony."

Mumba's work has significantly impacted the field, offering innovative strategies for fostering organizational harmony and efficiency. His contributions continue to shape contemporary management theories and practices.

www.ingramcontent.com/pod-product-compliance
Lightning Source LLC
Chambersburg PA
CBHW071828210526
45479CB00001B/39